10 0325799 9

AF741404

UNIVERSITY OF BRISTOL
UNIV[illegible]ITY LIBRARY
[illegible] AVENUE
[illegible]8 1TJ

D[illegible] [illegible]alled earlier)

MODERN INFLATION

Its Economics and Its Politics

Wilhelm Hankel and Robert Isaak

Science Center
Berlin

Pace University
Pleasantville, N.Y.

With a Foreword by

Karl Deutsch

Harvard University and Science Center, Berlin

UNIVERSITY
PRESS OF
AMERICA

LANHAM • NEW YORK • LONDON

Copyright © 1983 by
WILHELM HANKEL AND ROBERT ISAAK

University Press of America,™ Inc.

4720 Boston Way
Lanham, MD 20706

3 Henrietta Street
London WC2E 8LU England

Printed in the United States of America

All rights reserved
(outside of the German language)
including the right of reproduction
in whole or in part in any form

The German language rights are
held by the Bund-Verlag GmbH
Deutz-Kalker Strasse 46
5000 Köln 21, West Germany
which published the German version in 1981

Library of Congress Cataloging in Publication Data

Hankel, Wilhelm, 1929–
Modern inflation.

Translation of: Das moderne Inflation.
Bibliography: p.
1. Inflation (Finance) I. Isaak, Robert A. II. Title.
HG229.H23513 1983 332.4'1 83–12477
ISBN 0–8191–3383–3 (alk. paper)
ISBN 0–8191–3384–1 (pbk. : alk. paper)

UNIVERSITY OF BRISTOL

28 AUG 2025

WITHDRAWN

UNIVERSITY
OF BRISTOL

Dedicated to
the memory of
Sir Andrew Shonfield

CONTENTS

CONTENTS (continued)

CONTENTS (continued)

Foreword: A Step Towards a New Political Economy

Karl W. Deutsch
Harvard University
and Science Center Berlin

The international inflation workshop in 1981 at the Bologna Center of the Johns Hopkins University united scholars from the universities of Johns Hopkins, Princeton, Bologna, Florence, the Pace University of New York, and other centers of learning for a significant contribution to a crucially important topic. The ideas of Professors Hankel, Isaak and their colleagues deserve the careful attention not only of economists but also of all those interested in political science.

Like others, I have remembered since my student days my frustration at the ease with which textbooks and instructors of classical economics on both sides of the Atlantic invoked the alibi of "non-economic factors" whenever events failed to match the predictions of their theory. And since the fateful years of 1930 to 1933 I have remembered the danger of an economic theory that claimed that a great depression could be cured by deflation and unemployment and that was blind to the damage that its "economically sound" policies (coming after the earlier trauma of the hyperinflation of 1923) inflicted on the social system of Germany and many other countries. In its own way, classic economic theory often has been indifferent to the supposedly "temporary" and "necessary" human suffering that it produced and to the political catastrophies that followed.

The scholars at the Bologna workshop were trying to move away from the overspecialized economics of social indifference and eventual political disaster. Instead, they tried to trace the interaction of politics and economies and to keep the political and human consequences of economic policies in sight. These are problems that must be better understood if they are to be dealt with successfully in practice. A first step is to bring together economics, political science and sociology. But eventually there will have to be brought in also social psychology and the historical study of changes of human values, habits and patterns of behavior.

The Bologna workshop has not given us the last word on its topics. This seems clear to me, although I am not an economist. But my studies of economical nationalism and supra-national integration have brought me into contact with certain areas and members of that profession, and I have been engaged in research on ways in which modern political systems drift along or try to steer themselves in regard to a great part of their economic as well as political performance. Since 1976 I have been involved in developments of a computer-based world model, GLOBUS, at the Science Center Berlin--a model that is intended to simulate the interaction of political and economic processes at the national and international level. For all these reasons, I respect the scholars at the Bologna meeting and I welcome their efforts.

At this time we have every reason to support the attempts made at many seats of learning to renew and strengthen the field of political economy--indeed, to create a new political economy that will shed more light on these questions. The international workshop of the Johns Hopkins University at Bologna, by attacking the complex of inflation and of the public and private policies used or proposed to deal with it, has made a challenging and very worthwhile contribution to this task.

It is to be hoped that this initiative will be followed at other places, with the participation of additional experts from related fields of the social sciences. A broader and deeper knowledge of the economics and politics of "moderate" inflation--in contrast to the costs of runaway hyperinflation or, of deflation-induced stagnation--would be crucially needed, as soon as it could possibly be found. The old intellectual task of discovering whatever general regularities there are in the interplay of politics and economics--and what public policies might be derived from them--is being taken up again. It must not be abandoned.

--Karl Deutsch, 1983

PREFACE

Are the costs of anti-inflation policy higher than those of inflation? What are the distinctive sources of "modern inflation"? And which individual and collective strategies have been most effective in coping with the inflationary change of the 1970s and 1980s? These are the key questions addressed in this book.

This work has at least three fathers. Stemming from a friendship that began at the Institute on Western Europe of Columbia University, this transnational interdisciplinary collaboration between a German economist turned political civil servant and governmental advisor (Wilhelm Hankel) and an American political scientist turned political economist and management specialist (Robert Isaak) was completed at The Johns Hopkins University School of Advanced International Studies Bologna Center under the intellectual supervision of Karl Deutsch of Harvard University and Director of the Science Center in Berlin.

The U.S. Mission to the European Communities and the German Marshall Fund generously provided the contributors with grant support used mainly for an international Inflation Workshop held at the Bologna Center on April 29-30, 1981. The Workshop was dedicated to Sir Andrew Shonfield, whose sudden death made it impossible for him to fulfill his role of Chairman designate. Fortunately, Karl Deutsch was willing to assume this responsibility with his unique skills of interdisciplinary synthesis. The other commentators whose remarks upon the authors' theses helped to refine this work included Stephen Goldfeld of the Council of Economic Advisors to the President in the Carter Administration and Chairman of the Department of Economics at Princeton University; David Coe, an Economist at the OECD; Wolfgang Hager, a professorial research associate at the European University in Florence, Italy; Edward Weisband of the Political Science Department at SUNY at Binghamton; and Ahmet Aker, Stefano Zamagni and Vera Zamagni, professors of economics at the Johns Hopkins SAIS Bologna Center.

The authors are also grateful for the competent research, translation, and administrative help of Ronald Bee, Susanne Oechsner, Wolfgang Schill and John Schutte and, particularly, Janice Delbert--as well as for the assistance of the others at the Bologna Center. Sandy Greene did the polished final typing of the English manuscript. The German version of this book was published in 1981 by Bund-Verlag of Cologne, West Germany.

Wilhelm Hankel and Robert Isaak

PART I

INTRODUCTION

Inflation: A Case for Exorcism or Moderation?

(Wilhelm Hankel and Robert Isaak)

I. INTRODUCTION

Inflation: A Case for Exorcism or Moderation?

> At the bottom of all areas of scientific endeavor lie not the "objective" relationships among "things" but the "conceptual" relationships among "problems."
>
> --Max Weber (1904)

Who doubts that modern inflation threatens the political and social stability of Western democracies? Yet the threat exists not only <u>within</u> democracies, but also <u>between</u> them: not only are prosperity, the welfare state and the level of development placed in jeopardy; but the coherence of the world economy of nations, and their steps towards integration and progress are threatened as well.

Seldom have economic science and political practice been more united in both diagnosis and therapy: the bases of both the constitutional state and the achievement society have been thrown into doubt and inflation today must be fought more energetically than before to prevent further damage. It is even agreed that this should be done at the cost of higher unemployment; the only question is whether or not such unemployment is temporary or permanent.

Like the Sphinx, the ancient head that has guarded its secret up to the present, the riddle of modern inflation (the latest outbreak of perhaps the oldest money illness) keeps us guessing. The first mystery of inflation is that although we know literally "everything" concerning <u>what it is</u> (a process of continually rising prices; that is, of the falling value of money), <u>where it comes from</u> ("too much" money chasing "too few" goods) and <u>what it leads to</u> (that over time real income and wealth are distributed by chance and power rather than by performance and productivity), we still do not know <u>how to avoid it</u>.

For there is hardly a recipe for inflation-fighting or a technique for controlling the production of money which has not been tried in the two-and-a-half-thousand-year history of the use of money--all tried only to be thrown away eventually as useless. Whether it be the assumption of state responsibility for the currency or the removal of state control, whether the linking of money to rare and precious metals or its rigorous limitation in quantity through independent issuing or supervisory banks, whether legal orders to stabilize monetary value or clauses of contractual guarantee insuring the value of money, whether internationalization or nationalization of monetary policy--each of these means has brought us but one step closer to a unitary value of money as secure, incorruptible and timeless as the verifiable divisions of measurement on a ruler or a scale.

The real world demonstrates just the opposite: the "monetary yardstick" shrinks continually, despite all the efforts and attitudes of those responsible. In reality, output is measured differently from returns, the present is distinguished from the future, one currency is split from another and money loaned is separated from money borrowed. The penny and the farthing, which on the books of the medieval merchant were still a large unit of account and had what seems to us a fairytale-like purchasing power, can hardly find a coin slot willing to swallow them as a means of payment today. Instead, at the corner store in high-inflation countries like Italy, candy, chewing gum, and other small-change substitutes have largely replaced the fading pennies.

But who is really bothered by this unstoppable decline of real value and purchasing power of the monetary unit that transforms yesterday's medallions into today's small change, and the dollars and marks of today into the dimes and pfennig of tomorrow? Although inflation devalues the real income and wealth earned during one's lifetime and thereby damages the basis both of the market economy (where performance = productivity) and of the constitutional order (where a claim = a claim, no matter how long the interval between its beginning and its promised fulfillment), the society that set out to form predictable and just rules for the communal life of its members has yet to descend into the social jungle where chance rules rather than calculation, vitality rather than creativity.

And this brings us to the second riddle of the Inflation Sphinx: Although the inflation rate has continued to damage the productivity basis of the market economy and the principles of contract law, instead of bleeding from the wounds these institutions have been strengthened and further developed.* Although the inflation rate has raised unproductive speculation to a level of equal rights with productive investment and innovation as an investment alternative (often making it a more profitable alternative), the stream of social change and progress has never dried up, but, on the contrary, has become ever wider and richer. The inflation rate (which has existed ever since we have been able to grasp and measure it, however imperfectly) has continued to make every future more expensive than each preceding golden past, thereby working against law and order. Yet that which fathers and grandfathers managed to accumulate for their children and grandchildren by the sweat of the brow, these offspring have enjoyed with less work and more inflation than their forefathers.

If, therefore, the modern prosecuting attorneys of inflation (whether in science, politics or journalism) hit upon a similar cardinal point in their arguments, then it must have to do with their clients: the money-users, who were thought to be worse off with inflation (in all times and systems). The history of money and economics shows exactly the opposite to be true (except in cases of war-financed hyperinflation).

Therefore, we ask, must not the costs and consequences of inflation in modern Western society be considered differently and be given more weight than in previous studies of development? And if so--why?

Merely posing the questions in this way suggests precaution. Have we not also witnessed the public discrepancy between the feared and actual costs of inflation in contemporary society? Under the influence of general inflation-phobia, is not the goal of monetary stability given priority over equally important constitutional objectives of the democratic nation-state such as full employment, just distribution of real income and wealth, and the adjustment of the balance of payments? Or are these goals supposed to take care of themselves once inflation is eliminated?

---

*Inflation is an ever open wound never leading to death like the case of King Amfortas of the famous Grail, the medieval legend popularized in Wagner's opera Parsifal.

The achievement of these other social objectives will be neither easy nor automatic, even if the socially progressive, naive belief in Monetarism (that reincarnation of liberal, laissez-faire ideology) claims this to be the case. For tension between the primacy of inflation-fighting and other, not less legitimate, social goals is latent in any society which strives for both productivity and just distribution. But the conflict only threatens to break out when the "wrong" methods are used to work toward these goals--when a society like ours uses its numerous methods or instruments not to dry up the sources of inflation (in our case, the excessive production of liquidity which the monetary authorities cannot control given the "free" transnational credit market), but, instead, to aim at the inevitable symptoms of inflation: rising national prices and increasing private, individual protection of the money-user against the fall in monetary value.[1]

The social costs of misdirected inflation-fighting, which is for the most part ineffective in achieving monetary stability, are greater than the initial costs of the inflation rate itself. For under such circumstances the inner dynamics of the market and achievement society regress into risk-shy stasis, cutting down the range of freedom for progress and change in the legal order and reinforcing existing patterns of ownership.

The background and consequences of the deeply conservative-ownership characteristics of modern anti-inflation policies constitute a common interest of both authors: Wilhelm Hankel explores the theme of dynamic fluctuations between technical developments in money and in the means of production; Robert Isaak examines the equally dynamic strategic shifts of individual, corporate, and state money-users who must cope with the evolving milieu of the money economy.

Following an era that brought unprecedented real improvements in the living standards and in the leveling of all Western democracies--improvements unimagined by the authors of The Communist Manifesto over 130 years ago--the question that remains is why Schumpeter rather than Marx and Engels correctly foresaw the outcome of domestic class conflict. As he predicted, the mobile-property society has turned away from its own driving force--away from the affirmation of progress and change via risky undertakings (which includes accepting its prize but also its punishment). For in a society in which each actor or group is anticipating inflation--whether correctly or not--in the same manner (and percentage) only one thing is feasible: conservation instead of change. This is why an "unholy coalition" has arisen, a spectrum ranging from "left-wing" growth opponents to "right-wing" anti-inflation Savonarolas seeking to short-circuit almost every social cost through a not uncanny means--by the common disparagement of the dynamic basis of existence of our Western achievement and prosperity-oriented society.

In the prosperous Western welfare societies each person fears to lose something: hard-earned wealth and insurance claims, real income positions squeezed from closely fought professional battles, and so on. Literally everyone, therefore, is against inflation. Or, more accurately, almost everyone opposes it who realizes that the chance of loss stemming from inflation's ability to erode real wealth and income status will result in an "undesired redistribution."

If in the democratic spectrum of public opinion all poles of belief and value, from black to red, blue to green, come together as perhaps never before in the history of Western ideology to recognize inflation-fighting as the highest priority among social goals (even before the elimination of the domination of some men over others, whether at work or in society), then it is because they are obsessed too much by the "volonté des tous" (or "general will") of the "classless society," (which is classless only with regards to its common abhorrence of inflation). For such agreement has one predominant goal behind it: the maintenance of professional, economic and ownership gains up to the present, representing the basis of business as usual and legitimacy in terms of political understanding.

There could be no objection with this position were it not for two things: (1) Exactly those allied with this wealth-and-income-position motivated rejection of inflation are the first to come into contradiction with the law of survival of market economies, which requires dynamism and not stasis--dynamism not only in global growth rates but also in the rewards dependent on the productivity of individuals and groups which drive the dynamism in the first place; (2) Behind this disparagement of modern inflation an explanation or theory of inflation is developing that is highly dangerous because of its illusion of freedom of action for the "dramatis personae" acting on the monetary stage. This freedom of action has long ceased to exist in the raw reality of the world money economy. For no matter how well-grounded theoretically or how rigorously enforced, if the anti-inflation therapies (from tight money and super-high interest rates to exchange rate disruptions to austere budgets and union wage moderation) provide such disappointing and meager results as have the stabilization efforts of Western governments since the beginning of the 1970s, then the responsibility can hardly be borne by the men who did not have the courage to initiate unpopular policies. Nor by the facts that stubbornly refused to correspond closely with theory. Nor by the unexpected escalation of oil prices alone. But most likely, the fault is in the theories themselves.

No matter which style of modern inflation theory one selects[2]--the presumably outmoded Keynesian Excess Demand Model with or without the Cost-Push refinement, or the one-sided liquidity-oriented concept of monetary Excess Money Supply (which ultimately is not that different from the Excess Demand and Cost-Push models) --the predominant thinking of monetary policymakers rests on two central premises that do not correspond to reality: (a) that because of the dissolution of the fixed exchange rate links between individual world currencies (the abandonment of the so-called Bretton Woods Monetary System), each national currency area can determine the quantity of its currency offered on the market on its own and thereby can be free of the pressures of imported inflation; (b) that thanks to the free, transnational (Xeno or foreign) credit markets, which sprouted like weeds in the 1970s, an impartial, incorruptible currency appraiser has emerged which permits each currency user (and therefore every monetary policy-maker) to read how the infection of inflation has ranked his currency relative to others. So once the Swiss Franc and the Deutschmark, then the US dollar or, like Lazarus rising from the dead, the pound sterling took the title of world champion in the currency competition at different times. As a consequence, the managers of weaker currencies could presumably measure the appropriate anti-inflationary action or liquidity-reducing recipe.

One basic question was left open: what happens

if through credit the appraiser himself produces the currency he evaluates and in the process uses the resulting inflationary currency movements (from weak to strong currencies) to finance himself? No matter how one answers the question, traditional inflation theories and misleading anti-inflation therapies stemming from them continue unaffected on the assumption that there is and always will be a closed national currency area. They assume that it will be possible to seclude their currency greenhouse from the outer monetary world and to breed a non-inflationary financial climate outside the boundaries of the national quantity of money, a climate with an equilibriated system of costs of the use of money (interest) and of money exchange (exchange rates).

But what if these theoretical premises--these old ideas worked over anew and not necessarily related to the present--are no longer valid? What if, for example, the transnational money supply increasingly crosses national boundaries to substitute for the scarce national money supply? And what if the powerful demand for money on the transnational market determines its financing prices (interest and exchange rates) by itself? If this were, indeed, to be the case, it would be the first time in the history of money that the phenomenon of "world inflation" would no longer be made up of the sum of national, "home-made" inflations allowed to be exported into other currency areas as suggested by traditional inflation theories and therapies. World inflation would instead become much more of an unregulated, monetary No-Man's Land (an unsupervised bank of issue) beginning with the Xeno-credit markets and imported from there into the national currency areas.

How then is inflation transmitted? It is accomplished through the classical equalization of creditor-financed balance-of-payments deficits, not only in the Western but also in the Eastern and the Southern world (insofar as it is credit-worthy).

If in the world economy (the only contemporary "closed," though unsupervised, currency area) balance-of-payments deficits can be financed without the need for domestic adjustment (i.e., an increase in real exports), then it is clear that exogenously generated currency capacities beyond national jurisdictions are responsible for world inflation. Not only is there not a generally accepted theory at the moment designed to avoid this, but there is no appropriate instrument either![3]

Since our one-sided array of instruments cannot effectively fight this "modern" inflation now, or in the foreseeable future, we must ask ourselves how dangerous this inflation really is. Does it justify the suspicious zeal of its opposition? And above all, does it justify the gnawing fear of a reduction in social property status? For Machiavelli already noted in his Discourses (between 1512 and 1522) when examining the original Savonarola like an insect wriggling under his magnifying glass:

> Most often revolutions are evoked through the propertied classes, for the fear of losing awakens in them the same demands as in those who strive to acquire something.... Add to this that...their behavior towards the propertyless awakens the desire of the latter for property, either in order to take out vengeance for having been exploited or to be able to acquire wealth and position themselves, things which they see to be misusing them.[4]

Indeed, one would argue for "inflation permissiveness" or for Machiavellianism (without being unnecessarily horrified by the term), if one were to recall that in the two and a half thousand years of the history of money, inflation is the rule and non-inflation the exception.

Is inflation for that reason "normal"? The answer comes more easily if one conceives of inflation as a consequence of monetary economic progress for the benefit of all money-users (and not only of the money producers). For the expansion of the money economy and the reduction in the cost of producing money (thanks to the greater output per unit) are clearly simultaneous processes. Thus a straight path leads over the better use of scarcer and more expensive money raw material (precious metal) and over the disposal of cheaper money raw material (paper money) into cashless modern remittances and credit transfers. The increase in the velocity and the better use of money and credit capacity are overloaded to a degree that can hardly be measured any longer.

But, pure increases in turnover and better utilization of existing capacity in the transportation industry are worth little if goods are not moved and brought to the person who has a real need and use for them. Only with the possibility of money transfer are real resources exploited and real savings (that is, dead stocks) mobilized for the investment and innovation process which raises the collective productivity of the economy. This makes the progressive development of money socially useful. Therefore, the relevant question for everyone, particularly concerning the understanding of modern inflation is: Does a causal or functional relationship exist (not coincidentally in the lands and systems which have had a relatively advanced monetary and credit structure) between the "synchronization" of technical money progress and the improvement of real living standards? If so, what is the nature of this relationship?

Part II of this study attempts to provide an answer to this essential question. Wilhelm Hankel demonstrates that in one way or another each of the historically documented inflationary periods made social innovations possible which were difficult to finance and to introduce through other means. Rome's public (albeit thoroughly abused) monopoly of money production brought protection of the state and currency border for the first and last time in economic history: in the common market around the (Roman) Mediterranean there was a unified currency and price system.

The decentralization of the feudal system of seigniorage privileges strengthened the competing territorial authorities. It provided the necessary means of finance to permit them to lay an extensive local infrastructure (roads, canals and harbors), which later smoothed the way to a far-reaching market economy. The invention of private bank notes and credit creation consequently financed the construction of modern industrial capitalism.

Since, historically, banks existed <u>before</u> industry and provided every investment financing service, money played the role of a "veil" (Ricardo) for the classical economists; it rested above the real rates of production but did not stimulate them. With the linkage of domestic money circulation to the deposits and withdrawals of gold reserves (the gold standard) supervised by the central bank, the balance of payments in the 19th century limited the domestic inflation rate, acting as "the golden brake on the credit machine"

(Schumpeter).

In the "monetary nationalism" (von Hayek) of the 1930s monetary policy was to become the main actor in domestic demands for full-employment and for the "welfare state." The world economy was still more or less "disconnected." In the currency agreement of Bretton Woods (1944) a compromise was minted for the following quarter century between the new freedom from balance-of-payment adjustment pressures and the injunctions of the restored one world economy (through cooperation and coordination). In the post-Bretton Woods era of controlled floating exchange rates, the limited balance-of-payment credit available through the world currency fund (the IMF) was transformed into a new and more dangerous transmission-belt of world inflation via the free, transnational Xeno (foreign) markets.

What is the common denominator of this history in which any similarity is hard to find? An improvement of the money side through techniques of financing was always followed by an improvement so financed on the real side: with an increasingly plentiful and inexpensive money supply came growth in production and productivity, broadening the fixed boundaries of the redistribution of resources. But the temporarily excessive improvement in money technique above the real advancement in productivity always had to be "paid for" with an increase in the inflation rate. Yet even so it was always possible (albeit with some delay) to catch up once again with inflation's temporary lead through a combination of encouraging real increases in productivity and braking the progress of money-creating (bank) techniques through reforms in the money constitution. Out of the inflation-braking balance of payments of the 19th century arose the central (issuing) banks which regulated money circulation. After World War II these banks, in turn, were supranationally regulated, increasingly with the help of world central bank surrogates like the IMF, the "Club of Ten" national central banks with the hardest currencies, and similar international boards. In the meantime, since the abandonment of the Bretton Woods system and the oil price escalation, the "reserve-loss brakes" of the domestic and foreign inflation machine once again were disconnected: free exchange rates and free xeno-credit markets tolerate home-made inflation and finance almost every other foreign balance-of-payment deficit. According to modern monetarists, free xeno-credit markets not only appraise (inflated) currencies but they also transmit self-financed inflation world-wide.

The new laissez-faire international creation of credit, unique in the history of money, accordingly perforates the old, taken-for-granted scheme which assumed that any monetary challenge will be answered by a new round of real progress in productivity and a new and better money constitution.

The defensive battle against the world inflation of the 1970s and 1980s suggests a deficient therapy both in a constitutional and a real sense. Constitutionally, the unsupervised transnational credit markets should be integrated into the monetary system, if possible before the system's collapse (which we can no longer rule out). The collapse would be due to overdrawn production of liquidity which is actually "self-illiquidating" by freezing debtors in overdrawn positions. As this process continues a return of 1932 becomes more and more unavoidable. In the real sense, the need is (or was) for a firm new growth policy agreed upon by the Western industrial nations, and moderated by balance-of-payments tensions. The policy should be designed, if not to solve, at least to alleviate the inflation problem through expansion (increased supply of goods) instead of restriction (through drops in demand and employment). Likewise this should be achieved before an abandonment of integration or a loss of world-wide economic cooperation is brought about by a business/employment collapse which can no longer be dismissed lightly.

However, many problems present themselves in any rational attempt to lead a fight against inflation which promotes productivity and integration rather than deterring them. The greatest constraint is the domestic social pluralism which Dahrendorf accurately diagnosed as actually causing the decomposition of competition in the "consensus economy." That is, adjustment is no longer an automatic reaction to given prices, but is a negotiated bargaining and price-setting process in order to fix income shares. Therefore this pluralism has promoted the fixing of real income and property to the state of being the social program. This attitude operates as a constraint in that there is only one good way for the consensus partners to protect themselves against the unexpected inflation rate which they consider unavoidable. They anticipate the inflation rate and the limits it brings about by calculating it into their prices, contracts and projects!

Of course, modern social particularism, which has achieved the status of a distributing force, does not always beget the inflation that it subsequently prods the government and central banks to fight. But through its expectations or fears it strengthens and accelerates existing inflationary tendencies and thereby raises the costs of fighting them. Unfortunately the new costs fall upon the weaker groups on the fringe of society with fewer possibilities and weapons for self-defense.

On the not too distant horizon of aging Western societies an altogether new motive is visible for politically indefensible redistribution policies: the fact that old people lead a second, unproductive life after being pensioned off. This must be financed by the young, a burden which grows heavier because of the worsening lopsided proportion of elderly (the result of the sparse progeny of those to be pensioned). These circumstances make one of two things necessary sooner or later: either a huge jump in the productivity rate, or if that should fail to appear, a new distribution between pension and work income. Without one or the other the long buried class struggle will break out in the form of a generation conflict threatening the existential basis of modern society.

If in the past the redistributive capacity of inflation was mainly used in investment, in the future inflation could play an increasingly redistributive role in the relation between work income and the income of those no longer working. Thus inflation can also relieve the pressure brought to bear by the difficult business of politically unacceptable reforms by governments which are notoriously weak in regard to pension policies.

This is then the dilemma posed to the "self preserving consensus economy" by over-particularistic group power on the one hand and property-oriented, real-worth thinking on the other. This quandry does more than deepen the gulf and the tensions between the strong (rich and organized) and the weak (young, unemployed, etc.) groups in society. It does more than nourish the collective fatalistic inflation mentality through the prevalence of calculable expectations. The resulting mentality is far from harmless since it encourages rulers to employ some (incalculable) anti-inflation policy or other which, in turn, heightens social tensions rather than reducing them.

Even more important, the concept closest to the monetarist's heart, that of a society free of money illusion which is distributively neutral, ultimately leads to absurdity. Such a society loses the traditional advantages of money if the evaluation function of money for property, income and prices is linked to an index or other indicator of real worth. But it retains the drawbacks of the old pre-money barter economy. In the barter, or natural economy, the volume of real income of the individual as well as of the society could only grow. Higher output (due to higher worker productivity) or restricted consumption (that is, savings) makes surpluses of goods (or real capital) available. This real capital then makes investment expenditures possible as well as new rises in production and productivity. The advantage of the pre-money economy in terms of justice is that no one can raise his <u>own</u> real income at the expense of others; any single income can climb only when the individual in question (or someone on his behalf) works harder and/or saves more. Individual income and the gross national income grow either in step or not at all, so resource redistribution occurs either voluntarily (in the natural state) or not at all.

The disadvantage with regard to growth in the moneyless economy, however, is considerable: the producer and the saver remain, to a large degree, their own investors. The progress technically possible is stunted by entrepreneurial and sectoral "inbreeding" caused by generations of tradition-oriented rather than innovation-inspired investment by conservative farmers and handworkers.

Only with the introduction of the money economy can the producer and the saver, those people possessing property and tradition, finally give up their investment function. The new and unheard of chance to acquire real capital through money debts (credit) clears the way for a new type of possessionless but risk-taking entrepreneurial investor. He then can set up new centers of production and productivity outside and beyond the traditional sectors (especially new non-agricultural ventures). Only the money economy made the separation of the savings function from the investment function possible, bringing about the financial climate in which new ideas could be tested economically. People assumed the role Schumpeter labeled the "dynamic entrepreneur" without the use of their own earned, saved or inherited capital.

The money economy not only has invented the modern type of dynamic entrepreneur but continues to provide succeeding generations of the same type for society. Of course this will only hold as long as the money economy's light shines, with all the shadows it casts.

The monetarists, who have taken it upon themselves to save the world from the evils of money illusion and unearned redistribution through the inflation mechanism, themselves fall prey to an illusion. They seem to think that a distributively just, property-oriented society (through Index theory) has something to offer to the dynamic entrepreneurs and thereby might be able to solve our modern social problems. But what solution can it achieve? Neither full employment nor social equality, neither innovation nor structural change; indeed, it can probably not even solve the inflation problem itself, since monetarism always treats the symptoms and not the causes of the problem. The monetarists fail to realize that the non-money economy like the "ex-money economy" (given that it is stationary) always puts a premium only on the existing property status which prescribes its own form of justice to handle shortages and conventional property and role distribution.

In the money (and market) economy, on the other hand, the dynamic freedom of resource acquisition (through money or debts) triumphs over the static justice of the old owners of resources and the means of production. The money economy makes possible that which until today has been impossible: that real capital, above and beyond the amount stipulated by the real parameters of labor productivity and savings, can be formed and invested. This introduction of money also compels the (inflationary) redistribution of resources.

Inflation, in sum, plays the role of liberator in every phase of the developing process: the liberator of rights as well as of resources. It overcomes both the static nature and the property morality of outdated structures. By placing dynamism before traditional property rights, inflation taps society's reservoir of potential productivity for the most capable and daring investor. Moreover, through improvements in production and living relationships, inflation also changes society and the state more decisively and lastingly than all the revolutions thought up by ideologues (usually economic dilettantes) taken together. None have commented upon this with more insight than the Castor and Pollux of world revolution: Marx and Engels in their Communist Manifesto of 1948. If one replaces their epoch-conditioned term "bourgeoisie" with the more timeless concept we are analyzing, the point could not be better expressed:

> [it] wherever it has got the upper hand has put an end to all feudal, patriarchical, idyllic relations. It has pitilessly torn asunder the motley feudal ties...and has left no other bond between man and man than naked self interest, than callous "cash payment". It has drowned the most heavenly ecstasies of religious fervor, of chivalrous enthusiasm, of philistine sentimentalism in the icy water of egotistical calculation.[5]

It has, in one word, made chance calculable and the future financeable!

The problem is that the old system always tends to rebound. This occurs when the élan vital (vital impulse) of an epoch dwindles, or when the inflationary freedom of open resource acquisition and transfers is declared heretical and when the old feudal rights of property and established distributive justice are rediscovered (no matter how unjust this may turn out to be for the future). If the dynamic runs out at a certain time as it has at present in Western productive societies, or if the previous risk-taking investors and innovators begin to be interested more in protecting that which they have already acquired than in endangering it, then the preservation of property will again be written in bold letters and the freedom for change in the system with monetary (evolutionary) means will be relegated to small print.

It can of course come to the point where the new "justice" not only drives out the old freedoms, a form of legitimacy which protects acquisitions, but takes no account of that yet to be acquired, soon leading itself into absurdity. The principle "fiat justitia pereat mundi" is neither economically nor politically the better alternative in order to broaden the "limits to growth" in a way calculated to be (environmentally) clean. Such a restrictive principle also precludes the use of the constantly growing potential of human knowledge and ability in a productive way.

Like every social organism, the dynamic market and entrepreneurial society which permanently renews its own productive basis needs a "body temperature" to stimulate its functioning. But up to the present we have lacked clear and timeless means of measurement. We know neither the level of the normal temperature nor of the extreme temperature beyond which the organism can no longer survive (i.e. the 42° Celsius or 108.0° Fahrenheit of our society). The lack of an inflation thermometer which is compatible with the functioning of the constitutional state and market economy is, in reality, what makes inflation fighting so difficult. We do not know how much inflation is necessary to maintain the essential process of social, structural, and technical change; nor do we know what sort of inflation rate the modern property-oriented society can or even must be burdened with.

Precisely because the society of the future must live with and live through inflation just like the societies of the past, it is mandatory that the private sector reconsider its consensus economy mode of self-protection against the unavoidable climb of prices. Inflation protection begins at home. The second contribution to this study considers these instructions for living with inflation. Robert Isaak highlights the bewilderment of a society which, on the one hand, devotes itself to the conservative impulse and expects more promises than can possibly be kept, and, on the other hand, which constantly dilutes its commitment to self-help.

Isaak presents four types of private economic strategies designed to free the individual from inflation problems that have not been solved in the public sector. Their scenarios are played out at the level of the individual, of the firm, and of the state, ranging from self-defense to aggressive initiative, from short-term to long-term planning. These types are the modes of conduct of the Defeatist, the Free-Rider, the Maintenance Man and the Entrepreneur. Of course these "pure" types of strategies (which in any concrete situation are usually "mixed") are determined by their respective estimation of risk, time horizon, emphases, consumption habits, and their characteristic investment forms and habits.

From this perspective the inflation process plays the role of an "outside" social phenomenon (not influenced by the individual). It causes an acceleration of the tempo of life. This is not a consequence of inflation directly, but is due to its indirect redistributive effects.

In contrast, anti-inflation policies have a conservative, slowing, rigidifying effect. In this process, anti-inflation policies nurture a false consciousness of social amelioration, that is, a perception of less social conflict when the reality is the opposite. The unavoidable result is that the individual tries to increase his personal independence as much as possible. But by doing so he undermines any collective attempt to solve the problem politically.[6] Olson's famous thesis concerning the irreconciliability of individual and collective rational acts is exemplified by the case of self-protection against inflation. The so-called post-industrial society still preaches the concept of its forerunners--the virtue of precaution; those without means or work today still strive to provide for the future, but simply cannot. Instead, they fall into the roles of the Defeatist or the Free-Rider which results in their becoming a parody of the liberal promise of material self-sufficiency.

Even the Maintenance Man as a private or state manager is constantly compelled to make unholy alliances with the Defeatists and Free-Riders. This is because the pirates of the international credit-making cartel leave responsibility for the latter two types to those in Maintenance Man roles. And the dynamic Entrepreneur's behavior (the key to any long-term unleashing of productivity and the remedy for inflation <u>and</u> unemployment) will be discouraged both by risks that are now uncalculable and by the deceptive short-term security of the Maintenance Man. The money that could be available for progress-inducing projects with high productivity will be invested in a "dead-sure" but sterile manner.

Isaak confirms with a sociological assessment that which Hankel surmises economically: It is not the inflation rate that is the arch-enemy of the dynamic Entrepreneur, which more stimulates than destroys the productive and innovative forces of society, but rather the anti-inflation struggle which encourages the

Defeatists and the Free-Riders.

Thus anti-inflation rhetoric becomes the common ideological denominator for the medical diagnoses of all leading neo-conservatives. The survival of the poverty-stricken Third World countries rarely dominates the agenda of Western economic summits and business seminars. Instead we find the pension problems of rich senile societies which overburden their resources with taxes. If one initially feels threatened one drops the preference for democratic solutions like a hot potato. Not even the threatening energy bottleneck can break the type of joyous inflation financing that spreads so rapidly.

In short, inflation ends up stimulating the <u>ressentiment</u> of the rich, who envy the accomplishments of one another, much more than the exploitation of the poor by the wealthy. Already in the 19th century Nietzsche observed that a special feeling of envy, <u>ressentiment</u>, was becoming widespread in democratic nations, not that people begrudged one another their successes, but that they felt guilty for having surrendered before reaching their self-imposed goals, voluntarily, without real necessity. The Western promise of permanent progress and individual self-realization (exported to the developing countries only to make its claims even less fulfillable) collides with the socio-economic limits to growth, the inability of the productivity mechanism to get going again and the excess of public rewards for risk-shy behavior. Inflation not only raises prices; it also disguises social necessities and the social costs of adjustment with its mobilization of liquidity that is far too great. It does this in the realm of the individual as well as that of the enterprise, on the national level as well as on the international.

The <u>ressentiment</u> within the societies between rich and rich, old and young, and that <u>among</u> the societies of the rich and of the poor may be difficult to measure, but not to be foreseen. Yet without changing the <u>external</u> data, these <u>internal</u> problems of society cannot be solved. Until this change comes about, inflation will be used as a salve for these and other social wounds, as the lubricant of industrial development and as a veil behind which the money illusions hide from the all-too critical eye.

Can the Western welfare society be rescued from

increasing dependency upon the inflation drug? The common response of both authors, though shaded with different nuances, is that, unlike natural disasters, economic catastrophes can be avoided. One can foresee and analyze them and therefore can protect oneself from them. Thus inflation would only be dangerous and self-destructive if it did not always correct itself through the dynamic it sets loose. In this respect our society is no more "dependent" upon inflation than the body is "dependent" upon calories in order to maintain its own natural temperature.

Inflation only becomes dangerous when it approaches extreme dimensions--as in the case of nonsensical hyperinflation, or when it is avoided with the wrong therapy--as it is at present in most Western industrial states. In the first case the social organism collapses from overheating; in the second, from hypothermia induced by too much medication.

We need only to amend Lenin's famous stage directions on the self-destruction of the bourgeois society of 60 years ago, which Keynes since has handed down: "Whoever should want this, need only destroy its monetary system."[7] Add to this the clause, "and do it in the best and surest way available: through destruction of its potential for productivity and innovation in the name of exorcising inflation." For this creeping suicide, eliminating potential positive changes in the society, also prohibits any rational self-help actions on the part of the public--the private individuals trying to protect themselves from undesired effects of inflation. As Isaak shows it changes a society which at one time only rewarded the behavior of Entrepreneurs and Maintenance Men into one which goes so far as to reward risk-shy Defeatists and short-cut-taking Free-Riders.

Since the distinction between the fever found in sickness and the fever characteristic of recuperation is never perfectly clear, even for the most experienced doctor, only with the utmost circumspection will he prescribe forcing down the body temperature. Hot-cold treatments are better for the healthy than for the sick. The social doctor would do well to exhibit a similar caution. Even the social organism can withstand too high a temperature more easily than one too low; better no treatment than malpractice. For this reason inflation fighting is a task suited for moderation, not for operation. And certainly not for exorcism. In this light we hope that the following chapters will contribute to a better understanding of modern inflation.

FOOTNOTES

1. For a more detailed treatment: Wilhelm Hankel, Prosperity Amidst Crisis; Boulder, Co., 1981, p. 155ff) and Währungspolitik der unechten Sachzwange: DM-Starke statt Vollbeschaftigung, Kredit und Kapital III 1981.

2. The best overview available of the offering of logically seductive but socially meaningless modern inflation theories is Helmut Frisch's Die Neue Inflationstheorie, Grundriss der Sozialwissenschaft, Vol. 28, Göttingen, 1980.

The authors consider their studies as a complement to Frisch's presentation in terms of developmental, social and political theory. Frisch does a brilliant job of presenting the inflation mechanism and the possible theoretical ways of explaining it, but he leaves out the societal milieu of inflation (its social premises) as well as the societal impact (its social effects) as being plainly "meta-economic." In our opinion, however, neither the social premises nor the social effects of inflation are "meta-economic," rather they are precisely what one should understand and explain. Of all the present-day models of inflation, from Keynes to Friedman, as well as those of the past, which in various modes of interpretation are mirrored today in the "never-say-die" Quantity Theory of Money, none can be understood by itself. They are only understandable when placed in the context of their times and specific problems (and not infrequently, also the problem-solving intentions of the authors). These models, according to W. Eucken's famous distinction, may represent "logical" or even "timeless" theories, but they are not therefore necessarily "up-to-date" or relevant.

3. For a more detailed treatment: Wilhelm Hankel, "Wahrungsordnung bei weltweit ungeregelten Kreditmärkten?" in: Hans-Bernd Schäfer (ed.) Gefährdete Weltfinanzen Verschuldungsproblematik und internationale Finanzpolitik, (Bonn: 1980), p. 21ff.

4. Niccolo Machiavelli: Discorsi: Thoughts on Politics and Statecraft, German complete edition; translated, introduced and commented upon by Dr. R. Zorn, 2nd revised edition, (Stuttgart: 1977), Book I, Chapter 5, p. 23.

5. Karl Marx and Friedrich Engels, "Manifesto of the Communist Party" (New York: International Publishers, 1948) (100th anniversary edition), p. 11.

6. See Robert Isaak, _European Politics: Political Economy and Policy Making in Western Democracies_ (New York: St. Martin's Press, 1980) Chapter One and following, where it is shown that in times of overwhelming social change individuals in "post-industrial" Western democracies maximize self-interest and cede collective power by pushing social responsibility and policy options up to the superstructural level of governmental, corporate and union bureaucracy. They thereby make it even more difficult for the national political economy to adapt at the substructural level of political culture and values and at the infrastructural level of transportation communication and socio-economic work patterns.

7. John Maynard Keynes, _The Economic Consequences of the Peace_ (London, 1920), p. 220. "Lenin is said to have declared that the best way to destroy the capitalistic system was to debauch the currency."

PART II

THE CAUSES, HISTORY AND ILLUSIONS OF INFLATION

Wilhelm Hankel

I.

INFLATION - INTENTIONAL OR UNINTENTIONAL?

The Oldest and Longest Distribution Struggle: The Public Versus Private Sector

CAUSES, BACKGROUND AND ILLUSIONS

I. INFLATION - INTENTIONAL OR UNINTENTIONAL?

The Oldest and Longest Distribution Struggle: The Public Versus Private Sector

The modern inflation of the Western industrial countries since the end of the Second World War does not differ from its predecessors dating from the establishment of the money economy sometime in the "historic dawn" of the 6th or 7th century B.C. For some 2,500 years it has varied neither in its symptoms (rising price levels) nor in its consequences (the permanent reduction of already earned real incomes and property), but there has been a difference in its social evaluation.

Almost all previous inflation processes were--more or less consciously--intentional; that is, they were politically desired, although their initiators were far from having a systematic inflation theory. Up until the Roman Empire the states of antiquity "used" inflation, technically their monopoly on money creation, to finance their public expenses, from war to infrastructural improvements and welfare programs. This monopoly substituted for taxing power and was the normal way for states to finance public programs. The ancients perceived exploitation through inflation as far less disturbing than that achieved through taxation--although presumably just because they did not yet understand the connection between the government's act of creating money and rising prices.[1]

The feudal states of the Middle Ages also initially followed the tradition inherited from the Roman Empire. The only monetary and state financing progress in the late Middle Ages, the invention of public debt, developed from the practice of selling, or commissioning both the money-creation or "seigniorage" privilege and the public-owned gold and silver mines. Renaissance and baroque sovereigns used this range which the "public credit" extended for financing, that is, for the alimentation of the real public demand for resources, just as was done in ancient times.[2]

Until the middle of the 18th century the inflationary creation of money and public debt financed the first and longest distribution struggle for the real, limited national product: the struggle between the

UNIVERSITY OF BRISTOL

public and private use of real earned income and property. The mercantile and early industrial bourgeoisie which arose in the 17th and 18th centuries lacked a consciousness of inflation. This was most evident in the bourgeois revolts not against rising prices and inflation but against state and dynastic tax claims. England's "glorious" revolution of 1688-89, the Declaration of Independence in 1776 of the first 13 American states striving for equality in terms of taxation, and above all the French Revolution in 1789, which was directed much more towards equality than to liberty or brotherhood among the classes were all, in the true economic sense, "Early-poujadistic" anti-tax rather than anti-inflation revolts. "No taxation without representation" was their cry, though the tax burden then, compared to today's, was rather negligible, for both the individual and the entire economy.

Neither the leading economists of that time, the mercantilists nor the classics who fought and then replaced them, nor the great liberal state theorists of the epoch (Hobbes, Locke, Montesquieu, Rousseau) who promoted the idea of the constitutional state, diagnosed inflation as the negation of the right to private property which they themselves legitimated. In their conception of the ideal, good and righteous society (the "ordre naturel"), they perceived the only threat to this right to be the abuse of power and law-making, but never the abuse of money and credit creation (inflation). This abuse was so widespread that it broke all records in the age of bourgeois emancipation from the omnipotence of the ancien regimes.[3]

On the other side, the mercantilists who were oriented towards the state-guided economy convinced their sovereigns and citizens that inflation imported through surpluses in the current account is salubrious and that a rising state with a growing need for financing potential cannot get too much out of it.

After Hume and Smith unmasked this mercantilistic "money illusion" and asserted that society lives and prospers from its real goods (produced and imported), and not from nominal quantities of circulating money, they hit upon the next momentous error, the after-effects of which are still with us: The thesis that the circulation of money and credit influence only the absolute level of national prices and thus the purchasing power of national currencies. But not for long. For the famous "law of communicating tubes" holds not only for water, but liquidity, too. There is always a built-in ventile equilibrating differences in the (absolute) levels of national money supply--the balance of payment. Its surplus means increase, its deficit decrease in the national money supply.

In the new view of the classics, therefore, there was no space nor even chance for monetary policy, neither in terms of changes in money supply nor in terms of changes of foreign exchange rates. The latter had only the character of "metric" relations among currencies, equivalent to breaking down national money into units and sub-units (like dollars into cents or marks into pfennig). So, according to this theory, money (its change and movement) is lacking any distributional effects--nationally as well as internationally.

Hume's famous specie-price-flow model (or, more accurately, example) "proves" that the arbitrary doubling of the inflation rate in Ireland in comparison to that in England can alter the real terms of trade in the very short run, if at all, but never in the long run, and certainly not permanently. For the doubling of the Irish price level vis-à-vis the English corrects itself quasi-automatically in the shortest possible term through the reversal in the signs of the balances and therefore of payments too. Ireland becomes a net importer, England a net exporter. The resulting cash flow from Ireland to England and the equivalent flow of goods from England to Ireland balance the differences in money circulation and price levels with the "economic speed of light." With a given international volume of money (e.g. gold), inflation can only exist temporarily if at all; with free international trade in money and goods it cannot exist in a "real" sense.

And nationally, in the individual economy? Ricardo made the Hume-Smith judgment that in an internationally linked system, world as well as national inflation is temporary in character, institutionally waterproof. When, beyond the international volume of money (gold), a national paper money can be produced by private banks, national inflation cannot develop either: That is, if there is a link between private paper and public gold-covered money issuing by a new institution--the central bank. The volume of private money production is then tied to a legally prescribed gold value, making it nothing less than paper gold. These new rates, designed to neutralize the preconstitutional and pre-capitalist distribution struggle between the private and public sectors, ultimately stopped the greatest step forward in banking--using bank debentures (I.O.U.'s) as a means of payment (money). Inflation could only come about if--at a fixed gold price--the supply of gold in the world increased. According to Ricardo's "currency principle," which after Peel's Bank Act of 1844 until around the turn of the century was the basic model for English as well as most continental European central bank constitutions, things could become "dearer" only in the sense of <u>real</u> price increases, such as those occuring after a bad harvest. No inflation could develop in the sense of a swelling of national paper money supply.

Thus Ricardo redefined the constitutional framework, the ideal conditions for a <u>money constitution</u>, thereby making the new innovation of the banks--paper money--as good as gold. But in a deeper sense Ricardo transformed the famous Quantity of Money <u>Equation</u> (preformulated by Bodin and Locke) not only into a money <u>theory</u>, but into an operational guideline for money <u>policy</u>: not allowing the left side or "money component" to outgrow the "commodity component" (or the right side of the same relation). In this new ordered world of monetary stability, the price level (P) could only rise if real outputs (Q) fall, because the system was assured against increases in the volume of currency in circulation (M) and/or bigger fluctuations of its velocity (V).

The then nascent distribution struggle within the private sector between "labor" and "capital," a struggle which Ricardo indeed foresaw, and which Marx later derived from his theories, cannot in any case be financed by the internal inflation rate. The money supply is determined by the external balance of payments situation (withdrawal and injection of gold) and not by the internal profit and/or wage inflation. Internal income distribution is "technically" determined through the <u>productivity dependent</u> price and revenue relations, a theory which has been refined to the point of over-perfection by the "marginalists" of the later Vienna, Cambridge and Lausanne schools. The theory's main proponent was Walras, Ricardo's most devoted student. In his model of the closed barter system, Walras considered money to be the "numeraire" which changed barter relations into price relations. N goods have only n-1 exchange relations. With the introduction of good n+1 (money) all N goods will be measured by price relations expressed in money. But this new unit merely enumerates or indexes something which already exists in real terms: valuation differentials given by productivity (cost relations) and demand intensity.

That which Ricardo stated intuitively rather than proving analytically--that money is only a "veil" which covers the real production and distribution relations more in an obfuscating than elucidating way--was proved to be logically incontestable by Walras. However, in the social sciences, logical rigor is a necessary, but not a sufficient condition for proof. Walras's logic rested on a weak empirical foundation even during his time, preceding the outbreak of World War I. The argument is further weakened today, since modern inflation analyses, comprising major parts of monetarism as well as post-Keynesianism, refer directly or indirectly to Walras and Ricardo and their hypothesis of the "real neutrality of money."

Money, its volume, its price (interest), and most of all its preferential allocation through socially differentiating access to credit, have always had a significant impact on real production and real income, especially in times of credit-financed investments and innovation.[4] Since all scientists, not only economists, search primarily for the lessons of both tradition and their superiors (teachers), they almost automatically become "dogmatists." During their synods, they almost exclusively discuss theories and opinions of dissenters instead of real problems and conditions of the time.[5]

The great economists of the 19th century demonstrated this tendency by not thinking that the inflation problem had a "real" effect on production and distribution. Moreover, they thought the problem could be solved easily by adjusting the balance of payments and safeguarding the constitution, above all through the use of a strong, independent central bank. Therefore nobody developed an inflation theory adapted to the "progress" of inflation in transition from the 19th to the 20th century.

As depressing and nonetheless characteristic as this picture is for the present, it explains why science and politics were at a loss when a majority of the electorate in the Western democracies began, as they seldom had before, to ask unanimously for energetic, vigorous anti-inflation programs, disregarding its impact on employment. Helpless, scientists and politicians had nothing to offer but the old prescriptions, but administered in disproportionately stronger (and more dangerous) doses than before. They offered money supply quotas instead of money policy, disruptive rather than continuous interest policy, exchange rate volatility instead of stability. Since inflation can no longer be "intentional" or tolerated even to a small extent, scientists and politicians alike have to confess their inability to whip our inflation in spite of the massive application of the same medicine which was previously reliable.

This permits only one conclusion: We need new research on inflation which a) is free from the prejudices of older theories, and b) tries to analyze the changed institutional, structural, and social environment which distinguish this century from the last.

The nature of the inflation process itself (its origin, effects and transmission mechanisms) has changed since the 1800s when the classical theories were born that are still so respected. We can now turn our attention to the much more important question: How does inflation arise today and what can be done today to stop it?

II.

TWO DEVELOPMENTS IN THE PROGRESS OF BANKING TECHNIQUES

TWO DEVELOPMENTS IN THE PROGRESS OF BANKING TECHNIQUES

(1) Bank Credit Separates Itself from Money[6]

Money constitutions and state constitutions share the characteristic of having been designed as bulwarks against past crises and failures, not against those to come. Ricardo's "currency principle" is no exception. His proposal that the privilege of money creation be limited to a public central bank (which so impressed Marx that he adopted it as "Postulate No. 5" in the "Communist Manifesto" of 1848) was designed not only to protect the citizenry from inflationary expropriation by the money-creating state, but from the paper money production of modern banking as well.

However, the new problem of the epoch became the protection of the saver against expropriation by investors who were financing their endeavors with inflationary credits. Schumpeter's "dynamic entrepreneurs" would not have been able to finance any of their "Kondratjeff"-impelling innovations if the loss of the paper money-emission privilege had not led the private banks to realize the need for other, more significant innovations. Greatly surpassing the potential of their savings deposits, they began to refinance their customers' growing credit needs by taking out loans from other banks (interbanking credit lines).

Wicksell was the first to analyze this process of deposit-independent inter-bank liabilities, and described it in his book, which was revolutionary for modern concepts of inflation, Money, Interest and Commodity Prices (published first in German in 1898, but in English only in 1936). He concluded that this process of continuous credit inflation through the liquidity potential of credit markets is nearly unlimited. Since the markets constitute a closed system of automatic liquidity adjustment, given equilibrated expansion and business relations, the only thing which could stop this process of credit inflation would be unbalanced growth in interest and profit (in Wicksell's terminology: money interest and real interest). But that was exactly what was not to be expected according to the classical Ricardian-Walrasian idea of equilibrium. Since Wicksell did not participate in the classical underestimation of the inflation problem, he recommended a revolutionary goal in monetary policy: not the stabilization of exchange rates (representing the balance of payments) but the stabilization of the domestic price level. This theory marks him as the forebearer of modern price stabilization policy.

Since Wicksell's time, it is (or should be) clear that uncontrolled credit systems--even uncontrollable by the existing central bank instruments--have wide-ranging consequences. They not only autonomously separate the monetary component of the Quantity Equation (MV) from its commodity counterpart (PQ), but they also destroy Ricardo's stability norm. Of course, a connection between the rate of credit expansion and growth in productivity (real increase in Q) within a given time period does not exist, either logically or empirically, even though in the 1840s the banking school, vigorously fighting against the currency principle, believed they had proved such a link statistically.

Of greater importance is that in the free credit system complete separation of the savings from the investment function institutionally does more than just perpetuate the imbalance between factors essential to internal price and employment stability, thereby changing the exception to the rule in a dynamic economy. Schumpeter, in an exegesis of Wicksell, has pointed out this process. But the savings/investment split also means that growth is essentially an economic distribution struggle for the accumulation of real capital and assets.

In the old, static, pre-credit economy, the savers' surpluses determined how, how much, and for whom assets were invested. In the credit economy the investor's willingness to accept risk and indebtedness determines the kind of employment, income and savings potential that will arise. The prospective saver can decide how, how much and for whom he wants to save only to the degree that his income account, determined by the investor, will allow him to. He does not realize it, but his saving target is determined by the credit supply and the propensity to invest.

One of the unpondered bases of this system is that the savers agree with their deprivation of power, not to mention "exploitation," through the modern, uncontrollable credit economy--as long as they can fully realize their own subjective savings targets.

The situation only gets dangerous when savers have to fear either the loss of their ability to save (loss of job and income) or a reduction in the value of already acquired property. The Western world experienced a crisis based on the first case in the 1930s, and a crisis based on the second since the mid-1970s, when unfightable inflation increasingly threatened the existent stock of financial assets, as well as the permanently growing income and savings potential of non-investors.

In other words, only in a crisis, be it unemployment or the absence of steady prices, will the inner instability of a free credit system which is beyond the control of money constitutions reveal itself. Only then will those who are stricken by the crisis demand action--action which cannot be achieved by "mere" democratically legitimated governments without dictatorial authority. In 1930 no government could command its bankers to abstain from credit contraction, since it is also part of the "Wicksellian Process" to run in both directions. And today no governments, whether unilaterally or in concerted alliance, can loan the xeno (foreign) credit markets.

The permanent financing of oversized current account deficits of otherwise "rich" industrial countries, unstable East bloc countries, and a number of developing countries which hope to become productive in the future, actually represents a substantial contribution to world inflation (as every responsible person knows). In all deficit countries this policy fixes nationally excessive expenditure, price and cost levels, but any cessation of this "external deficit spending" would immediately and abruptly intensify the national crisis.

So one thing can be said about the state of modern inflation without prompting accusations of ineptitude: Although the mass of voters in all Western industrial countries both rejects this inflation rate, which is in part self-accelerating, and measures their government's success by pursuing its impact on the inflation rate, the governments consider this same inflation to be the lesser evil. Inflation postpones the huge, momentous unemployment crisis which would occur as automatically as it did in the '30s if there were no inflationary compensation for the accumulated deficits in current account (whether they are caused by the price of oil or not).

Though nobody in a responsible government position would admit it, the current inflation is at least _tacitly_ "intentional."

The reason is clear: the former advocates of abundance are themselves hardly resolved to preach ascetism. Moreover, the affluent would not be very credible preachers, trying to convince others to bear hard times while they themselves wallow in wealth. We may wonder whether communism, which shares capitalism's materialistic goals of affluence, can resist the appetite for success once it gets a taste of it. (See Hans Jonas: _Das Prinzip Verantwortung_, Frankfurt, 1979.) The answer was evident even before the events in Poland: a resounding "no!."

Charles Maier's verdict that Keynesianism in the '30s overcompensated with internal inflation until the war industry healed all wounds (his "conservative illusion") in order to solve the contemporary structural and employment problem of high capitalistic societies is therefore repeated on the global economic level 50 years later.[7] The deficits which then appeared in the national budgets are now found in (largely private) current accounts; they are not financed by _money_ creation any more but by international _credit_ creation. In the '30s, the public inflationary policy was welcomed with relief by the private sector, while today an essentially private inflation is welcomed by the public sector, which can now neglect additional national activities.

The stage has changed but the play is the same. It would require a "strong," that is _un_democratic government to drop the play from the repertoire.

(2) The Perfect Credit System of the Modern Xeno-Markets: The OPEC Example[8]

Ever since xeno (foreign or "stateless") money and credit markets came into existence, people have argued about them. For their apologists they are the contemporary zenith of banking progress, the perfection of the pure credit system which is totally independent from both the real saving process (deposits of the so-called "non-banks") and the credit creation control of the central banks which, in effect, "govern" through their currency monopoly and reserve requirements. For their critics, these markets are a pure "inflation machine."[9]

Actually they are both. The credit expansion of the banks behind all this now has to be measured in <u>trillions</u> of U.S. Dollars and has already outgrown by far the concurrent real expansion of world trade. Since 1973, the beginning of currency flotation and oil price escalation, the process has continually picked up speed.

A look at Table II-1 and Figure II-1 bears out our contention that since floating began the Euromarkets have in fact financed national exchange- and interest-rate disturbance and instability rather than real world trade and capital transactions. Both numerical values demonstrate clearly that since the beginning of floating the "financial" turnover rate (Eurocredits) have continued to increase more rapidly than the "real" turnover rate (world exports). Since 1974 nominal world exports increased by one-third (real exports by far less), while the Eurocredits rose threefold. These figures, better than all the more or less mythological bank models, clearly show that Euromarket self-financing is not only not declining but is on the increase. But they also show that the once strict connection between the balance-of-payments deficit of the United States and the growth of these markets no longer exists. The assumptions by all the volume analysts of both the older and more recent schools about strict and constant relations between money base (i.e., U.S. balance-of-payments-contingent U.S. dollar drains) and Eurodollar credit increases no longer obtain. As Table 1 shows, the U.S. dollar drain due to current balance-of-payments deficits between 1965 and 1972 amounted to approximately 50 billion dollars, while new Eurocredits stood at approximately 120 billion dollars. Between 1973 and 1977 this relation went up, from a balance-of-payments deficit of 52 billion dollars to a Eurodollar credit creation in the 525 billion dollar range. The original relation of 1:2 of the sixties rose to 1:10 with a continuing strongly rising tendency.

The credit creation of the Euromarkets operating on the international scene thus emancipated itself from its source of primary dollar liquidity--from the United States. The federated system of the Euro, Asian, Pacific, and Caribbean banks today works like an independent nineteenth-century private national or central

Table II-1

World Liquidity and World Trade
(in millions of U.S. dollars)

Year	Currency Reserves	U.S. Balance of Payments	Euro-Credit Volume	World Exports
1965	70,719	- 1,280	14,210	
1966	72,300	+ 219	18,330	
1967	74,053	- 3,418	24,850	
1968	76,928	+ 1,641	31,830	214,300
1969	78,214	+ 2,739	58,330	245,500
1970	89,472	- 9,840	78,250	282,100
1971	124,976	- 29,739	100,130	316,600
1972	117,907	- 10,313	131,840	367,200
1973	118,343	- 5,353	188,600	524,200
1974	146,110	- 8,821	214,120	773,400
1975	158,415	- 4,712	442,400	794,300
1976	182,105	- 10,470	548,090	907,000
1977	204,287	- 22,512	657,300	1,030,000
Reported:				
1965-1972		- 49,991	+ 119,620=1:2.4	
1973-1977		- 51,868	+ 525,460=1:10.1	

Sources: IMF, International Financial Statistics, Washington, D.C.; Bank for International Payments, Basel.

Figure II-1

World Trade and Xeno-Credit Markets

1970 = 100, logarithmic index

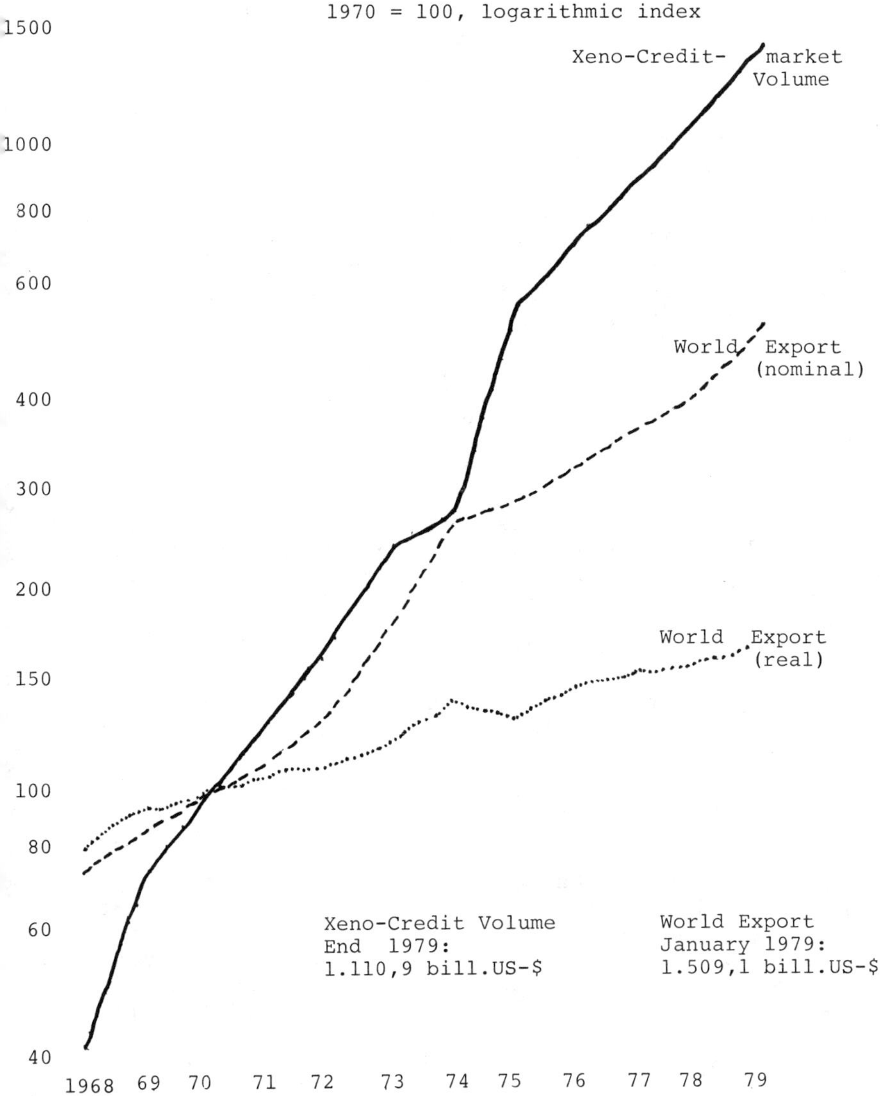

Source: Figures for world export from IMF, International Financial Statistics, Washington, D.C.; for Eurocredit volume, from Bank for International Payments, Basel.

bank system, which refinanced practically 100 percent of its credits through self-created bank deposits (interbank debts) and notes (certificates of deposit). This interbank system creates the previously described world financing framework that allows countries to weather balance-of-payments deficits and take their time about the necessary, painful adjustment. Thanks to this deficit-financing the surplus countries can also take their time; they can permanently export more as well as refrain from otherwise indispensable financing activities (capital exports). In other words, the credit-creating abilities of the free international money or credit markets preserve the reserves not only of the deficit countries but of the surplus countries as well. As to the deficit countries, the new credit markets simply help them gain time, for they must repay their debts eventually. In the case of the surplus nations, the flows remain a part of their reserve, for thanks to the Euromarkets they neither require as much monetary assistance as in the past nor do they have to finance capital exports out of their own reserves.

As Table II-1 shows, the "official" reserves of all IMF members more than doubled between 1970 and 1977, from less than 93 billion dollars to more than 200 billion dollars, almost exclusively in foreign exchange (or U.S. dollar) holdings, which more than tripled during that same period, from 45 billion dollars to more than 158 billion dollars. But even more important, the outstanding Eurocredit volume increased almost tenfold, from 78 billion to more than 657 billion dollars; both these amounts of international liquidity can legitimately be added, because they protect the reserves of both deficit and surplus countries.

The Euromarkets obviously have become a far more powerful inflationary mechanism than the Bretton Woods system in its late phase. If one compares the reserve growth of the sixties with that of the early seventies, the new inflationary mechanism shows a tenfold increase in the credit-creation multiplier. Moreover, this mechanism is no longer served by central banks that at least officially are not directly involved in purchasing. They allegedly still rely on the dividing effects of floating (however inconsistently they may handle it) and are literally blind to the inevitable inflationary consequences of the increase in reserves in surplus and deficit countries. Moreover, this permanent over-production of the alternative (or Euro) dollar and alternative reserves permanently finances its own slumps (in U.S. dollars) and booms (in strong Eurocurrencies). This occurs ultimately because of the basically senseless (and for the United States dangerous) 1:1 relation between Eurodollars and U.S. dollars, which makes it possible for every self-legitimating currency valuation to percolate through to the U.S. dollar with the economic speed of light. Those who continue to insist that the United States is responsible for its own dollar weakness are only half right. For it is not generally U.S. domestic overdemand or inflation that sets off an oversupply of U.S. dollars, which depresses the free U.S. dollar rate vis-à-vis other currencies, but an oversupply of Eurodollars that depresses the U.S. dollar. What is right is that the U.S. government itself is at fault for allowing this link by the private banking sector between the U.S. and Eurodollar to continue instead of cutting it.

Perhaps the President of the United States or his successor will echo the sentiment voiced by Hjalmar Schacht in the thirties, and the next time a European or Far Eastern visitor complains about the weakness of the Eurodollar will say to him: "Why are you telling me about the weak Euro or Asia dollar? That's your dollar, not ours. Ours is the U.S. dollar, and since it, like all normal currencies, is floating vis-à-vis the Eurodollar, you as well as we can tell more readily how much it is really worth."

As early as 1977 competent observers of the Xeno-markets estimated that only 8% of the total credit volume served for the financing of imports, exports and real investment. Thus 92% served for purely speculative transactions: currency movements, exchange rate speculations, the so-called "hedging" at the forward market--all transactions within what Keynes called speculative money, M_2, in contrast to the money he considered necessary for circulation, that is transaction M_1. This is a functional definition which is distinct from the formal monetarist definition that M_1 represents cash and M_2, money in the bank. If indeed the Xeno-markets finance "everything," both the "necessary" (real transactions) and the "burdensome" (currency fluctuations), it may disturb national money officials because they have lost control over credit privileges. But does this automatically imply that inflation is nourished? Is it not true that the currency fluctuations which the xeno-markets indeed _finance_ but do not _incite_ are _the consequence_ of existing inflationary tensions and disparities, not the cause?

The problem becomes much clearer when we look at the effects of xeno-credit financing: no country, whether an industrial, East bloc or developing country, suffers losses in its currency reserves corresponding to its level of xeno- or foreign credits. Therefore, no adjustment in the capital account is necessary. Keynes's dream for this Bretton Woods system was to free the debtor countries from the deflationary duty of capital accounts adjustments, a duty which is not only troublesome, but also dangerous for the employment situation. The xeno markets have made this dream a reality in a totally unorthodox way which would upset rather than please the later Keynes. The modern world economy with built-in global xeno-credit markets automatically finances virtually all current account deficits (whether caused by oil price increases or not) much like a clearing union, without any built-in limits on credit or obligations for a hard currency policy. The only condition the markets and the banks behind them require is that the transactions be "reasonable" (micro-economically profitable)--as if there had ever been a shortage of such even in the most encumbered East bloc or developing country.

As a consequence, countries with a high deficit in the current account (with national "consumption" higher than the national product) can preserve or raise the already permanently climbing cost and price levels as well as the national spending rate. _External_ credit co-finances the _internal_ inflation rate without effect on reserves and the balance of payments. We want to show how world inflation is created and transported from the outside into national arenas ironically not in spite of, but because of flexible exchange rates. Therefore we will use the OPEC example (not the least because of its statistical clarity) as a _pars pro toto_ to trace the process of the perfect, all too perfect, recycling of money from OPEC and other sources.

The OPEC current account surpluses have swollen greatly since 1973 and are reflected in their capital balances which have since become debit accounts. This could be seen as experimental proof of what Keynesian theory still maintains today. This theory--rejected by the monetarists--has provided the explanatory hypotheses for all "closed systems," independent of inequivalencies in and pressures on the balance of payments which would disrupt the national full employment and price stability policy. In the financially integrated world economy of the '80s no system is as "closed" as the world economy itself and nothing so "national" as a balance of payments. So Keynes's General Theory from the '30s is unrestrictedly applicable today, 50 years later, only for the analysis of world economic problems. In the national economy, however, it must be supplemented by a multitude of "ifs" and "buts."

A rising oil bill has a profound effect on real income which is used for consumption and investment on the domestic level. If, as in the 1973-1981 period, the oil-importing countries have to pay considerable, ever-increasing sums in the billions for oil (1980: $80 billion), thereby transferring funds to the accounts of oil producers, their real incomes will dwindle. The money will flow into sparsely populated "oil and sand states" which can spend only a fraction of their budgets for domestic consumption and investment. Thus only an even smaller fraction of the original amount (a fraction of a fraction) returns to the "exploited countries" in the form of OPEC orders for additional consumption- and investment-dependent imports. "Real" recycling through an automatic increase in exports to balance the higher oil import costs is distorted, basically because the surplus countries' capacity to absorb is structurally too meager.

As difficult and problematic as it may be to calculate exact figures for the rates of absorption or income dispersal in the oil producing or exporting countries, we can be sure that they are lower than those of oil consuming or importing countries. If we take Y_N as national income, C as national consumption and I as national investment, national absorption can be calculated as $A=Y_N-(C+I)$, divided by Y_N to make it a percentage. If now--as a consequence of the OPEC current account surpluses--a permanent redistribution of world income (Y_W) comes about from industrial and developing countries with a high A to OPEC countries with a low A, C+I must decrease outside of the OPEC

UNIVERSITY OF BRISTOL

area. The drop in C affects nearly all developing countries and the drop in I affects the richer industrial countries. Furthermore, world income (YW) does not grow anymore--or in any case grows more slowly than it would have without OPEC surpluses and income redistribution. Why?

If we assume for a moment that Y_W would be unaffected by a decline in consumption and investment in developing and industrial countries, it would mean that the difference between world income (Y_W) and world consumption (C_W) obviously increases. But this difference $Y_W - C_W$ is essentially world savings (S_W). If S_W increases more than world investment (I_W), which in the non-OPEC states is constrained to their limited absorption capacity, Keynes's famous condition for an under-employment disequilibrium is fulfilled. In other words, the Y_W redistribution from countries with a high A to countries with a low A leads automatically (i.e., in the absence of countervailing actions) to a real world slump, because the existing and planned world investments (I_W) fall behind the existing and planned world savings (S_W): $S_W > I_W$.

There are many consequences of this ex-ante balance between S_W and I_W which investors in the non-OPEC world generally did not plan for. A gap grows in domestic demand due to a lack of disposable income in the industrial and developing countries. Existing production and employment opportunities cannot be fully used any more and at least a partial depression and unemployment crisis occurs.

If we do nothing, or do the wrong thing, against this process it will continue until Y_W has sunk so deeply that S_W and I_W balance again. But this point where $S_W = I_W$ is at a level where great parts of the world's capacity for production and employment outside of the OPEC area must lie fallow. Why does this result?

It would be inevitable because this equilibrium point requires that OPEC's (partial) additional savings are compensated for by smaller savings in other parts of the world. In other words, the more the OPEC states increase their share of Y_W and S_W (which used to be easier for them, thanks to their autonomous oil price policy), <u>the more the non-OPEC states have to slow up</u>. Their Y_W must sink (or rise more gradually than OPEC's) until their diminished savings (their renunciation of growth in Y_N and I_N) balances OPEC's additional savings. Only then could a world economy which is left to itself calm down and regain a balance with considerable under-employment--and that only under the condition that OPEC countries then refrain from a further maximization of their claims on world income and savings!

Keynesian income analysis also explains what happens on the world money markets. The OPEC states, as already mentioned, have an almost absolute preference for liquidity, in terms of currencies, securities and other means of investment. They invest their savings which they took from the non-OPEC states, either in extra-short-term investments or demand deposits in their own banks, which for the most part must credit them in generally accepted currencies such as Petro-Dollars or Petro-Pounds.

As a consequence, not only these banks, but also the xeno markets where they usually operate, find themselves under permanent pressure on investment and interest rates. Based on their permanent over-liquidity those banks and markets which are haunted by the OPEC funds can undersell any national level of interest, naturally only to the degree prescribed by competition. If, for instance, the national money institutions follow a super-restrictive policy to cool down the domestic inflation rate and expectations, as the U.S. did in the first half of 1980, they bestow upon the OPEC investors an extra, unexpected "interest gift": The investments remain liquid but collect agreeable earnings even at the minimum level of national super-interest rates.

The permanent over-liquidity of Petro-Dollar banks and markets not only leads to permanent competition pressure on the national credit conditions, but also forces the national money institutions permanently to pursue exaggerated policies if they want to have any effect at all on their domestic markets. We will later explain what structural effects and costs this leads to in the long run using the "model of stability," West Germany.

What does the Keynesian world economic analysis, briefly outlined above, make clear to us?

First, it does not leave any doubt about the fact that the OPEC surpluses have primarily a deflationary, and not an inflationary effect on the national cycles of OPEC-oil-dependent countries. They are forced painfully to adjust the rates of internal growth, employment and the standard of living.

Second, it also makes clear why "real" (import-export) recycling is incomplete and why "financial" recycling fails. The OPEC states, because of their liquidity preference, are not interested in compensating completely for their current account surpluses (T, for "Trade Balance") in their long term capital accounts (CA). The major part of their current and permanently increasing T surpluses (+T) is not balanced by a deficit in their capital account (-CA) but through highly liquid private reserves (+R). Since (+T) $>$ (-CA) there is a permanent increase in (+R).

This leads to a third conclusion: Since the majority of current OPEC worldwide savings is invested in external bank liquidity (instead of real investments), the OPEC banks and markets acquire an enormous and powerfully competitive potential for credit creation and inflation. OPEC thus behaves as a worldwide transformer of long-term real capital (investments) into short-term money capital (bank deposits), and produces a worldwide surplus of money capital over real capital creation (based on its "crazy" investment policy): a world surplus of liquidity.

By this time a fourth conclusion is apparent: The xeno-banks and markets which manage OPEC's reserve portfolios play a game which is dangerous for the world economy as well as for themselves. They have produced credits out of liquidity for a long time, year after year, at an ever-increasing pace. In this way they are trying to roll back the OPEC policy of shortening financing deadlines, an attempt which is economically rational for the world and national economies, but one accompanied by considerable credit and liquidity risks for the banks involved. We will later come back to the aspect of "safety in operation" of this system.

The conspicuous difficulty for xeno-banks and markets, however, lies in the fact that they themselves do not have a statistical overview of the total existing and constantly growing OPEC assets. They know only their own OPEC accounts, but not those of their competitors, whether in banking or other fields of interest. Furthermore, they are compelled to compete, just as they are compelled to invest. They must expand their business in order to stay in business. In short, we have to consider the fact that their active dynamic exceeds their passive dynamic as a functional law of the petro-dollar markets. They bridge the "liquidity trap" of the OPEC states not only with credit intervals, but also with credit volume. The xeno-markets produce more additional credits yearly than OPEC furnishes in the form of world savings.

How do we know that? We can only estimate it according to available records which are incomplete. The annual reports of the Bank for International Settlements from 1973 to 1980 show, for example, that every year the loans from xeno-banks were higher than the increase in reserves of OPEC states held by private banks and public agencies. Considering the inadequacy of these sources we should pay less attention to the specific annual surplus of credits over concurrent OPEC savings than to the "opening scissors" trend represented.

But if all xeno banks in aggregate issue more credits than the only apparent secure and stable world creditor, OPEC, offers as the capital and deposit base (after deducting its own credits), then the surplus of world credits over world savings is pure "inflation potential." This holds true even if we do not know exactly in what parts of the world or in which goods and services production processes it will become most virulent.

Is the trend to world inflation therefore OPEC's fault? Is it the consequence of OPEC's favorite creditor policy, preferring liquid reserve accumulation at the xeno-markets to a real investment policy vis-à-vis its deficit counterparts? The latter at least would have balanced the oil price induced deficits and surpluses on current account in the capital instead of the reserve account.

Our world economy analysis makes clear that, fifth, OPEC does not contribute to threatening world inflation, though it is doubtless OPEC's fault that we are simultaneously endangered by world depression. It

Table II-2

Xeno-Credit and its Refinancing
(in billions of U.S. dollars)

	1975	1976	1977	1978	1979*)
I. Outstanding Xeno-Credits (as of year's end)	428.1	523.3	650.6	836.3	979.0
Industrial Countries	257.9	324.0	405.4	530.8	616.1
Eastern Europe	21.6	28.8	38.3	47.5	52.8
Third World	63.0	80.9	98.7	121.7	147.2
Off-shore & unclassifiable	67.6	89.6	108.2	136.3	162.9
II. OPEC - Reserves	37.5	40.1	38.8	26.6	44.4
III. OPEC Reserves: Xeno-Credits	1 : 11	1 : 13	1 : 17	1 : 32	1 : 22

*) for September 1979.

Source: Bank for International Settlements, 48th and 49th Annual Reports, and Provisional Report, February 1980 - table respects the remarks contained in the original sources. (the ratios are rounded off)

would be miraculous, however, if this OPEC partner could accomplish even this without the help of his own banking system partner. No, the world inflation is solely the fault of the system of xeno banks and markets dominated by the West. The guilt is shared by the entire *dramatis personae*: those who carry out the process (the Western banks) and those who up to now have refused to regulate it (Western governments and central banks).

What if one were to assume that the world creditor OPEC isn't necessarily satisfied only with *private* bank debts (his own deposits) to cover his reserves, e.g. debts to national central banks, or even to a world central bank (which unfortunately does not yet exist)? Not only would the total available volume of OPEC savings be abruptly shown statistically, but also the central banks would know what amount to release in order to compensate for world-depression effects. Furthermore, they would know when we are about to reach critical inflation thresholds which could easily be avoided. The deposit of OPEC reserves in the central bank system would prevent the worldwide credit and deposit creation which has committed the xeno markets to the highly inflationary Wicksellian process, a process that only can stop with one thing: a catastrophe.

Unfortunately, the subject is not yet dead. In the other, larger liquidity pool of the xeno markets, the highly speculative M_2 (in the sense of Keynes, not Friedman), there also lurks a possibly more explosive inflation potential. This functions with the mechanism of speculative exchange rate fluctuations, i.e. changes in the terms of trade, or changes in import/export prices. To the degree that this speculation causes devaluations, terms of trade worsen, and very strong cost-push effects appear, due to the concurrent opportunities to finance imports.

On the other hand, if this speculation causes currency appreciations, it improves terms of trade and has no restrictive effect on surplus countries. This is due both to the deficit countries' ability to finance their balance of payments deficits and to the possible price level shifts. Thanks to the inflation difference between themselves and their deficit markets, the surplus countries can preserve and even improve their export volume, as West Germany did in the 1970s.

Thus the surplus countries not only export inflation *into* the world economy through their monetarily improved terms of trade; they also simultaneously import inflation *from* the world economy because of their partners' excessive spending level, which is financed by the Euromarkets. A circle of reciprocal inflation cause and enhancement results: The debtor countries "save" themselves the painful deflationary balance of payments adjustments, thus bearing internationally too low a rate of inflation which for them, however, is too high. Meanwhile they are importing more and more permanently financed inflation.

The financing potential of xeno-markets literally makes "everything" possible--currency speculation, the transfer of increased export prices of surplus countries in international currency. This not only overrules the internal adjustment process of the debtor countries, with the help of increasing exchange rates. It explains the "miraculous" development which would seem to contradict the lessons of history: Today exhorbitant appreciation rates do *not* imply a curtailment of export and competitive capacity (consider again the example of West Germany).

We can see, therefore, that, when examined closely, there is no contradiction between the arguments regarding the "blessings" and those regarding the "curses" of the xeno-markets. Indeed, these markets have a problem-solving function; they can equalize any payments imbalances more or less silently, e.g. those between oil importing and oil exporting countries and those caused by the consequent recycling. Nevertheless, while performing this function they may have a highly inflationary impact. In fact their inflationary impact actually leads to their problem-solving function.

For example, given certain money illusions in the domestic cycle (*intra muros*), it is not too difficult to finance wages safely which are in reality too high. This is accomplished without effect on employment by expansion of money volume and higher government spending--Keynes's recipe for overcoming the national employment crises of the '30s. In the same way it is possible on the international level to finance a spending level which is in reality too high without effects on employment and balance of payments as long as there is a sufficiently large volume of credits.

The only objective not met appears to be keeping the process neutral from inflation. For this exactly is the essence of crisis-solving through the financing potential of the xeno-markets: National spending levels, excessive when measured against the GNP and balance of payments, are always maintained, and therefore back real balance-of-payments adjustments in the form of more exports and less imports.

This is a completely new and unique situation brought about by the destruction of the Bretton Woods system. Although this system, called the "perfect inflation machine" by the late German central bank president Blessing, was destroyed in order to avoid imported inflation, it has been replaced by an even more perfect inflation machine. It is a "crisis solver" which enjoys the benevolence of all governments anxious about balance-of-payments equilibrium and full employment. These governments court the xeno-markets, even though at home they repeat again and again that they are enforcing the strictest anti-inflation policy possible.

The only weak excuse for this political hypocrisy, which today exists in all western industrial states, is the schizophrenia attributable to the monetarist wing of economic thought. The monetarists condemn the policy of improving the employment situation with a little fiscal inflation as <u>national money illusion</u>. But at the same time they adhere to a much more dangerous <u>international money illusion</u>, according to which free credit markets and free exchange rates are the straightest (and only) way to avoid inflation, as if the ideological prefix "free" outweighed the odium of misconstruction in a flawed mechanism. This is a tragic error which could be laid to rest if only Hayek and Friedman were a bit concerned. Unfortunately for the rest of us, it has political consequences.

III.

MONOPOLISTIC COST-PUSH
OR
FROM PRICE ADJUSTMENT TO EMPLOYMENT ADJUSTMENT

(Schumpeter's Vision of the Self-Destruction of Private Capitalism Today)

3. MONOPOLISTIC COST-PUSH OR: FROM PRICE ADJUSTMENTS TO EMPLOYMENT ADJUSTMENTS

(Schumpeter's Vision of the Self-Destruction of Private Capitalism today)[10]

The modern methodological dispute about the proper way of combating inflation--a controversy which has developed over the years between "orthodox" Keynesians and monetarists--brings to mind most of all a form of mature scholastic conceptual semantics. Most Keynesians adhere to the right side of the quantity of money equation and divide the total aggregate national product into its component parts, or the withdrawals for consumption, investment and exports. If the current total expenditures for all partial aggregates are higher, the real disposable national product brings about inflation; the price level must climb. The monetarists adhere to the left side of the same equation and declare the volume of money to be the greatest inflation inducer and trade parameter (as a precaution they resolve the velocity of money circulation into a harmless calculable constant).

What neither orthodoxy ever seems to see clearly enough is that, under both of them, the "real side," the Gross National Product, and its components including its calculable rate of change, sets itself up as a given on the money side. The money side must adjust to the real side and not the other way around!

Whether according to Keynesian excess demand theory or monetarist excess money supply theory, inflation always implies that the GNP, which is curiously considered "real" under the fictitious prices of a year long passed, lags behind the sum of expenses for consumption, investment and exports. Money expenditures are too high compared to the available supply of goods and services and therefore increase prices and the margins for price increases. Price increases bring about a cost-push. The margins for price increases then allows the cost-pressure to pass to another sector so that, thanks to the demand surplus, the price spiral can continue to turn without an obstacle. The process occurs simultaneously on the national and international levels. The country which is at the crest of this wave drags along the other countries with its import surpluses (the export surpluses of the others). This is especially the case if the country has a so-called "economie dominante" (dominant economy), whose currency has a reserve asset character and is bought by other countries or their central banks.

For years the USA was the archetypical proof of this theory. The American balance-of-payments deficit, enhanced by strong deficits in the capital account, greased the monetary demand mechanism in almost all other Western industrial nations. Though the USA's domestic inflation rate stayed behind the world average until the beginning of the '70s, according to this theory the country exported too much liquidity due to the balance-of-payments deficit (mainly caused by the capital account deficit). This, in turn, encouraged growth in the money supply throughout the world. The consequence was that worldwide interest rates could never reach the level of "deterrence" which Keynes postulated as necessary to preserve money value stability. This theory is popular not only because it is in accordance with outdated textbook concepts, but also because it confirms the most venerable of all economic cliches, namely that of the omnipotent demand-supply mechanism which supposedly could be applied to even the most highly complicated macroeconomic problems. Finally, the theory is also politically useful because it exonerates the national governments: The inflation is imported and not homemade.

If the demand-supply theory were right, the naive therapy which it requires (aiming to cut excess demand until demand and supply balance again) should have been successful long ago. Since the abandonment of the Bretton Woods System of fixed exchange rates liquidity has not been imported anymore. Instead it has been rationed by national currency and economic policy according to strict standards. Since then interest rates reach temporary peak levels unlike any seen since ancient times and the Middle Ages. The main factors behind the Keynesian inflation process--profits and new investments--declined because of these hard monetary conditions in all Western industrial nations. Nevertheless price increases and cost-push continued to exist until finally the latter surpassed the limits of the former, profits turned to losses and the boom became a world-wide depression.

Why? Obviously because supply and demand are not separate from one another, but are mutually related variables. In all Western industrial nations the same basic process generally takes place: each restriction on demand by governments or central banks sooner or later also restrains the supply--the old imbalance is perpetuated at a lower level of employment. Figure III-1 elucidates this connection.

The employment and price levels E_1 and P_1 exaggerated here which result from the supply-demand constellation S_1/D_1 are to be reduced to the "healthy" employment and price levels E_0 and P_0. According to the obsolete prescriptions demand is reduced until it falls to D_2. If supply were to remain unchanged, the new supply/demand constellation S_1/D_2 would lead to the optimal price and employment combination P_0/E_0--the stabilizing policy would have reached its goal. In reality, however, the reduction in demand brings the supply schedule down to S_2. With the undesired supply-demand constellation S_2/D_2, the old excessive price level P_1 is preserved while GNP and employment fall beyond E_0 to E_2. The new balance combines the old inflation rate with a reduction in GNP, and most of all with the new addition to unemployment, E_0-E_2. We must therefore explain why measures to restrict demand which are undertaken by governments and central banks (credit restriction, fiscal frugality and flexible exchange rates) have an effect on the supply schedule of the economy.

It has been (or should have been) clear for a long time now that the modern (nominal) wage/price system is only flexible in one direction: up. Nevertheless, this aspect is still being largely ignored in inflation theory and policy. As an increasing percentage of those offering either products (enterprises) or manpower (unions) react with *price* instead of *quantity* adjustments when confronting the demand restriction resulting from the rising cost and dwindling supply of credit, *the problem of unexpected excess supply arises for all monopolistic price and wage fixers*!

The *entire* deficiency in demand can no longer be offset given prices and wages fixed at higher levels. The problem can be expressed in another way: in a monopolistically stiffened price and wage system, *the real adjustment of prices and wages* which is predicted by theory and expected by politicians either does not occur any more, or it occurs to too small a degree. As a result, the market process, "sterilized" by the

Figure III-1

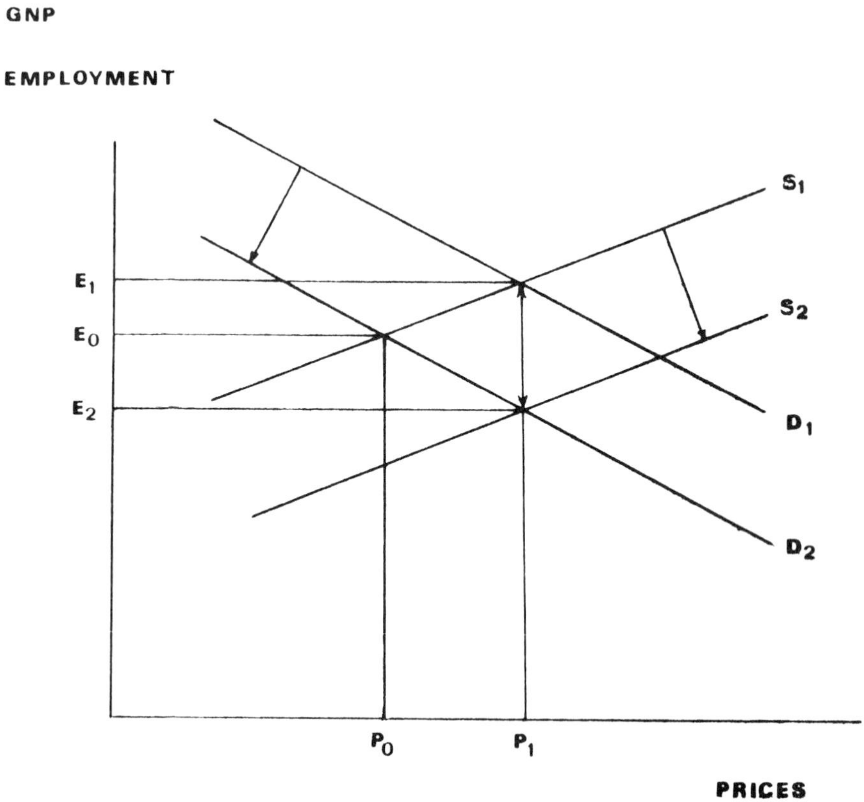

inflation rate, makes the real adjustment of supply necessary, i.e. the quantity adjustment of production and employment.

Behind this change looms the altered investment process. According to the still unrevised perceptions of present economic and currency policy-makers, this process continues to act in the "classical" way: Many small- and medium-scale enterprises (very few large-scale), none of which have a unilateral influence on the market, calculate each investment individually, without considering the aggregate investment position of their enterprise. Before deciding on a new investment, they compare the expected additional benefit with the additional costs in financing. If the expected net return is positive, they contact a benevolent banker and borrow the necessary funds. Even if they do not need credit financing, they make a marginal cost-benefit analysis for the planned project to find out whether they would be better off investing their capital in their own business or somewhere else.

The "classical" view is outdated in two essential ways: First, in almost all sectors of developed countries, the majority of investment decisions does not take place in small- and medium-scale enterprises. Instead these decisions are made by large firms which take on the role of "branch leaders." For a long time now the structure of modern industrial goods markets has been partly oligopolistic, and in areas of high capital intensity it becomes more and more purely oligopolistic. The big enterprises in each branch of industry determine their means, size and tempo of investment almost unilaterally, while the small and medium firms must behave as investment-adapters.

Second, big enterprises usually do not evaluate projects singly, but evaluate investments in the aggregate. Since they share the belief of territorial states that they are immortal, they have also adopted their budget methods, although the firms have made two important improvements. They do not plan for one year, but calculate their cash flow in terms of the internal accumulation of capital and external financing possibilities (availability of credit) for several years.

With this changed financing behavior comes a refinement of their reactions to external financing conditions dictated by money officials. A shortage of liquidity and a rise in interest rates has only financial effects on big enterprises; they do not change investment policy. A multi-year investment program is not cut back or cancelled just because necessary external financing becomes more expensive over a longer term. The financial experts of these companies have a variety of options at their disposal. They can switch over to short-term financial markets, lower programmed depreciation quotas for awhile, or--ultimately, ratio-increase prices. The oligopolistic nature of the modern investment process with its methods of accounting which keep financing independent of specific projects, allows the integration of financing costs into the production costs to an unprecedented degree. Externally restricted liquidity and high interest rates resemble a financial tax and become a fixed part of the enterprise's calculations. Financing costs are transferred into prices as are external taxes and internal costs (wages and materials).

If now demand is restricted, it follows that instead of bringing the same supply to the market at lower prices, firms will offer a lower supply at the same price. This is all quite possible for the various branch leaders given their oligopolistic market position. As price leaders, they fix the margin for price increases for the entire field.

To avoid misunderstandings, we should note that the oligopolistic structure of growth industries and technical progress industries is not merely some regrettable mutation, a degeneration of the market system which is therefore correctable. It is rather the necessary consequence of investment expenditures inevitably climbing per production unit from one innovation-push to the next, a price for progress first pointed out by Joseph Schumpeter.

The increase in investment costs is composed of two augmenting factors. First, the investment capital input per production unit and/or per worker increases permanently for technological reasons and due to accelerating wage increases. Second, investment intervals are continually shrinking. Out of the progression of investment pushes which were tied to an investment cycle evolved a smoother, continuous investment curve with a constantly increasing tendency.

The unavoidable consequence of the inevitably rising price of investment is that a firm has to maintain or if possible even extend its market share at all costs--even in times of tough governmental restriction policies. Only then will the nearly incalculable investment costs and risks be hedged to a degree by price changes. The acquisition and defense of oligopolistic and monopolistic market positions has become the condition sine qua non of progressive capitalism.

IV.

THE WELFARE STATE FEEDS ON ITS OWN CHILDREN

From the Class Warfare of the Poor Society to the Generation Conflict of the Senile Society

4. THE WELFARE STATE FEEDS ON ITS OWN CHILDREN

From the Class Warfare of the Poor Society to the Generation Conflict of the Senile Society

It is a common platitude that "poor" developing countries have societies with "too many children" and that "rich" industrial nations have societies with "too many old people." Oddly enough, however, as a consequence both of them must strive toward the same goal to solve their diverse problems. The poor countries strive for economic growth to provide more jobs than before. The rich nations also need economic growth, but for the purpose of producing more real income to support the living standards of their old people who are no longer productive. The latter is a new and ever more threatening challenge to the economic and social policies of modern welfare states.

According to Malthus's basic assumptions, the population of a given political economy grows more rapidly than its economic output (or national product). Although this configuration holds true today increasingly only in developing rather than industrial countries, conventional economic thought still preaches it with important implications. If the assumptions hold, all economic progress (i.e. in the real rate of productivity, no matter if the additional product is employed in terms of labor or capital) should lead to the improvement and enlargement of the employment base.

The formula: the greater the production, the greater the employment _solves both the productivity postulate and the justice postulate_. _This is the obligatory task of all societies regardless of their ideological formation_ (whether democratic, communist or authoritarian); _it is also the measure of a society's worth_.

The recurring speculation that the population in theory could grow more quickly than the economic potential required for its occupation and subsistence has important consequences for economic and ideological thought in our century. It blurs the characteristic split between classical (i.e. conservative) and Keynesian (progressive) welfare postulates and measures. The supposition that a higher real rate of productivity or growth solves, or at least evidently defuses, almost all social or distribution conflicts, unites, rather than divides, all anti-Keynesians, irrespective of their orientation or shading. In this respect modern economic theoretical disputes about the proper way to prolong the favorable growth rate resemble their theological forerunners of past centuries concerning the surest road to heaven. Both conflicts are literally disputes over little more than an iota. The Keynesians have "faith" in the indispensible anti-cyclical function of state intervention in forms from deficit spending to encouragement of investment, to structural policies; while monetarists and other anti-Keynesians have "faith" in the indestructable elan vital (vitality) of the private sector which, driven by the profit motive, tends by itself toward the complete utilization of existing economic potential. Both theologies argue about the most appropriate and shortest way to the gates of heaven. The commandments of the productivity-oriented meritocracy and those of the justice-oriented social state are reconciled over the maximization of production and employment.

Laboring under the prejudices of this goal, if not also of their conception of methods, these theoretically and ideologically opposed churches of modern Keynesianism and monetarism both worship what Charles Maier called the "conservative illusion." This is the contention that a growing real per capita income can heal any social wounds of earlier eras and systems with time, hardly leaving a scar, regardless of what sort of distribution struggle caused them. We have already seen that the credit apparatus, with its nearly infinite preparedness to supply necessary, cheap means of finance, strongly aids this process.

But what if the real per capita income continues to grow, but this time only in aggregate terms (that is, before but not after the social corrections of money withdrawn to finance the social or transfer income of progressively growing (rather than productively earned) old-age pensions?) If, in other words, per capita income is only climbing because the population is falling relative to economic potential instead of rising?

This is no wild-eyed, hair-pulling prediction of a negative utopia. Instead it describes a future which has already begun and which, according to the average phases of generative behavior familiar to us from the past, will last until deep in the 21st century. One need only consider the extrapolation of the aging population development of the two core western industrial countries: the USA and the Federal Republic of Germany. These cases may be considered typical and representative for all western industrial countries which are culturally and demographically homogeneous.

A commission of experts described the demographic future of the Federal Republic of Germany recently in the following terms:

> Germany finds itself at present in the second phase of a long-term decline in productivity. The first phase stretched from the '80s of the last century to the beginning of the '30s of this one. The second phase began in the middle of the 1960s. In reflecting on the causes of the current low productivity value it is unlikely that this value will rise through self-regulating forces to a level of reproduction in the near future.[11]

The same contracting trend in the U.S. population is confirmed in a recent parallel study by A.F. Ehrbar.[12] He contends that, as in the Federal Republic of Germany, not only will the aggregate American population stagnate or even recede a little, but for our analysis a much more serious problem will emerge. The proportion of active, working people between the ages of 15 and 60 will shrink and the proportion of inactive old people will climb sharply.

Therefore, a dramatic displacement of the traditional demographic proportions will occur in the wealthy countries of the west (no matter what meta-economic and economic bases are used to define these nations). Within the next two to five generations, the old will outweigh the young and it follows that the non-working population will outweigh the working. This leads us to the question: What consequences does this have for attitudes toward claims on economic and social policy?

The basic attitude of a society growing "senile" is static, or property-conservative: that which was attained in earlier working life should and must be preserved. Just pointing out this shift indicates the profundity of the desperately straw-clutching fear of inflation, not to say inflation-hysteria of the modern western society. It goes beyond the special, traumatic experience of the German society, which twice in the first half of the century suffered hyperinflation as a result of cynical war financing, gambling on the "final victory." Today's fear is a general expression of the anxiety of aging people approaching the autumn of their lives.

Since the elderly predominate both in numbers and in position, they (and not the young) not only set the tone in our democratic systems, but also represent the majority of the voting potential (the volonte des touts--or "general will"). Therefore the political response of voter-dependent parties and governments "must" at least pay lip-service to inflation fighting, regardless of what they may really think of the probability of success of such a policy.

The about-face of former West German Chancellor Helmut Schmidt is particularly revealing on this point. Still in 1972 as Minister of Finance he declared, "I consider 5% unemployment to be far more dangerous than 5% inflation." But two years later, as a head of state determined to stay in power, he turned his earlier slogan on its head and introduced a policy of "better 5% unemployment than 5% inflation." The resistance of his own party notwithstanding, he enacted this policy and thereby defused the explosive domestic political demands of his forerunner Brandt.

Schmidt's exemplary conversion from an ideological Keynesian of the old school--conjuring up full employment at the price of "a slight bit more inflation"--to a practicing monetarist for whom avoiding inflation has become the precondition to full employment, stands for a new variety of "conservative illusion". This version holds that an appropriate economic and social policy (one which is eliminating or reducing inflation) can maintain the constant growth of per capita income of the aggregate society uncurtailed as the operating base of social and redistribution policies.

Precisely this base, however, is acutely endangered by the persistent self-destruction of the demographic balance between young and old! This is because the young and working sectors of the population, independent of the prevailing system (or non-system) of social security, are always the real financiers of "unemployed" old-persons' incomes which are no longer earned through the recipient's productivity.

In this instance, if in no other, Ricardo's metaphor of money as a veil which obscures rather than illuminating actual relationships finds its meaning and justification. For the worth in real purchasing power of these old age costs, derived from current income and consumed by the aged today, will tomorrow (that is, after one or two more decades) depend not on one but on many unknown factors:

- The future proportion of the working compared to those no longer working (the proportion of aged);
- the future volume of the real GNP (the basis for assessment);
- and the individual cost of living allowance which a future society will award to its non-productive retirees after taking into account the whole of its growth, distribution and stability policies.

A much simplified model may clarify these basic relationships. We signify the number of old (non-working) people with A, the number of young (working) people with W, the real per capita income or per capita national product the working sector produces with Y, and the living allotments of the aged not yet guaranteed by social insurance programs, with P (for their individual pension incomes). This clearly leads to:

$\frac{A}{W}$ (= proportion of Aged) X $\frac{P}{Y}$ (= pension burden) = b wherein b is the computable individual burden of pension costs, i.e. b represents the portion of the per capita income Y earned by the young which is needed to pay for the P of the old. With other words, the less favorable the proportion of aged becomes ($A > W$) and the higher the pension burden (the nearer P approaches Y), the higher b, the individual burden, necessarily becomes. The young, at the expense of their "earned" per capita income Y, increasingly finance the "unearned" pension income P as b rises. This follows from the fact that $A \cdot P$ (the total of all pension income) can be financed only with $Y \cdot W \cdot b$ (the total of all workers' income multiplied by the burden or income redistribution coefficient b).

There is just no getting around the fact that the real encumbrance of the old, the real income level of pensions, is paid for by the (earned) per capita income of the young and working generations. <u>The fruits of labor of the young and not the acquired or putative capital and insurance claims of pensioners once active both make possible and limit the real standard of living of the aged!</u>

Thus the above mentioned Y, hard-earned by the younger cohorts of the population, will continually diminish by the factor "b" calculable from the equation. The well-known German social scientist Mackenroth has formulated this concept and lent his name to it. He laid the theoretical foundations for Adenauer's (a successor to Bismarck's) newly regulated and dynamized (income-indexed) post-war social insurance. The Mackenroth view is that "all social contributions of a given period must be defrayed and financed out of real earned income or the national product of the same period."

With certain marginal exceptions (enumerated by Buchanan among others) there are neither temporal (that is, intergenerative) switching yards, nor financial exoneration mechanisms (in terms of capital) in the income-transfer budgets of nations.

The means of financing these demands is almost of secondary importance. If the aged use up the financial assets they have saved (interest and capital), they are only aware of the nominal worth of their payments, not the real worth, which is dependent on the unknowns mentioned above. If they meet their needs from their individual or social insurance policies, then, although the presumedly professional fund management guarantees a certain nominal degree of protection against risk, there is again no <u>real-worth security</u> in their payments. Technically the only secure real-worth source of income for the unemployed aged is that already found in most continental European social insurance systems, namely the financing of pensions through <u>governmental income redistribution</u> (compulsory premiums, taxes). This policy of financing pensions, which can still be considered to be rational, is more or less able to come to grips in advance with the first two unknowns through its insurance technique. But the extent to which the policy can also fine-tune the third, more important unknown, i.e. the ability of the working population to bear the burden of maintaining those who no longer work in times of a "lop-sided" proportion of the aged, is the real question we are about to take up.[13]

Given space limitations we can only highlight the particulars this implies. The income-redistribution factor b which we use to measure the burden of the aged will grow the more the proportion of aged shifts away from a preponderance of the young and working. It will take on "momentous" proportions not only for social policy, but also for the entire economic policy in general. It will do this in three overlapping and cumulative ways:

FIRST, even without policies, the real old-age burden is escalating because of the explosion of life expectancy.

SECOND, an additional aggravation is that in the meantime almost all western industrial states no longer permit their "b" to be determined in a "natural" manner (on the basis of the prevailing birth and death rates). Instead they determine it in a socio-political manner. Modern social insurance, whether based on the strictly automatic German model, or on the much looser U.S. model, always portrays an attempt <u>to fix the value of "b" politically</u>. Whenever the natural old-age burden (A:W) is combined with the political fixation of the pension burden (P:Y), as in the West German social insurance program, the burden on the income of the young from the living standard of the old (our "b") <u>becomes a variable politically dependent on the entire system and its policies</u>!

The following figure (IV-1), duplicated from official documents on German social insurance, demonstrates where this trend will lead. Extrapolating from today's situation, the burden of real old-age income in the case of the Federal Republic of Germany will double from about 25% to over 50% in the year 2030!

Figure IV-1

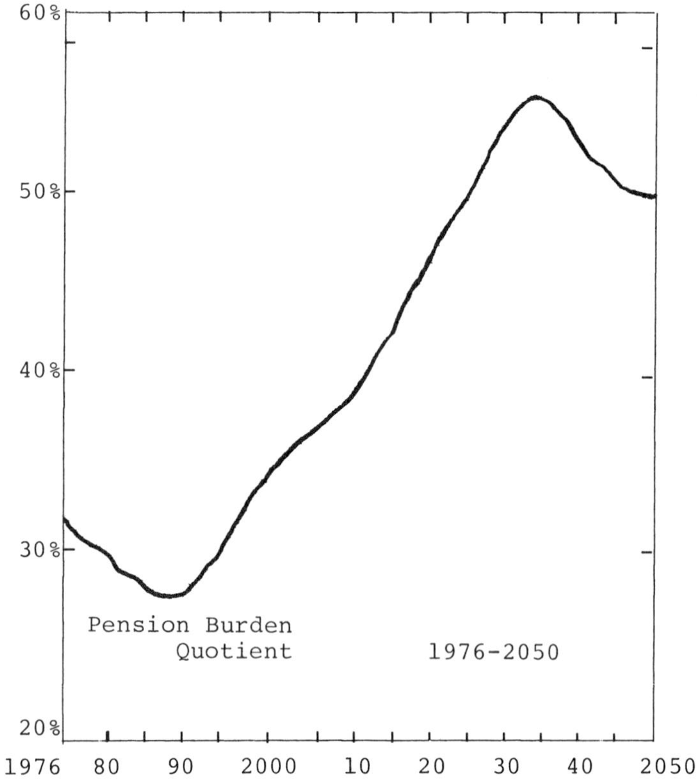
60%
50%
40%
30%
20%
Pension Burden
Quotient
1976-2050
1976
80
90
2000
10
20
30
40
2050

In addition, in the case of the Federal Republic of Germany, the portion financed by the "openly" acquired (or directly levied) "b" is shrinking from year to year. In each budget the newly acquired national debt contains a larger share of deficit financing for the support of social insurance. The tendency is apparent: democratic politicians, dependent upon the will of the voters, will solve the problems of old-age burdens and income redistribution as long as it can be done in their more or less inflationary way. They do not reduce "b", but instead *they transfer its financing from the direct, visible methods of premiums and taxation, to the indirect and less noticed technique of loan financing*.

The German national debt, which at about a third of the present national product has certainly not reached its inner limit, will increasingly be used as a financing technique to disguise the real burden of old-age security. The same politicians, who at the insistence of their "senile" constituencies have put inflation fighting at the forefront of their efforts, are increasingly turning to finance this goal in an inflationary way. *The intervention of progress in banking techniques in the otherwise openly threatening distribution struggle between work and recent idleness (young vs. old) makes inflationary financing possible, as it does for so many things!* The slogan used by the opposition in the election of 1980 about the government's "pension betrayal" unfortunately possesses fatal meaning and nuances when looked at in this light!

Nevertheless, it was the official defender of German social policy, the Chairman of the Federal Ministry for Employment and Social Order (Professor Meinhold) who warned the old and new governments:

> Were we [the government] to raise the pension adjustments constantly according to the present formula with a doubling of the old-age burden quotient ... and were we to change nothing else, especially not the social contribution law, then we would be forced [and are, in fact, already today!] to increase the contribution rate from the present 18% to 36% of gross worker earnings alone for pension insurance.

It is hard to determine whether the observer's use of the subjunctive was meant to express hope or resignation!

THIRD, the final way in which the old-age burden is taking on momentous proportions has long been ignored. It casts an even brighter light on the structure of the modern welfare state oriented toward generative assymetry: while old-age security is a duty of public income redistribution, the covering of the youth burden remains, even after the decline of the large family, the responsibility of private finance. According to an opinion poll published in 1979 by the Council for Family Affairs (using 1974 as the reference year), the monthly expenditure of the average family in the Federal Republic of Germany was DM 1,251.00 per child under 15 years. The contribution of public transfer payments for this purpose amounted to DM 176.00 per child monthly. The deficit left to private financing therefore amounted to DM 1,075.00! This will hardly stimulate the willingness of the young to take over further old-age burdens in the long run.

These few remarks prove that the democratic decision-making mechanism is as unfit as can be to solve this problem. In most Western societies the aged (and those about to become aged) already largely represent a decisive voting potential. Therefore, both real security of old-age pensions and stability of money value (i.e., anti-inflation policy) become the dominant election themes in the mentality of the "senile" society. Add to this the presence of party competition in all Western systems, and the political offerings of the various groups seeking office narrow themselves more and more to these two focal points. Instead of a choice among political alternatives, the voter is ostensibly offered higher degrees of realization of the same program. Political debate degenerates into a sterile dispute over disingeneous basic position, specious alternatives and frequently personalized verbal radicalism.

This is the real and unfortunately justifiable reason that the resulting narrow, one-dimensionality found in the party platforms disgusts both the critical and the young voters. Of graver consequence still is the fact that "income policy designed for the aged" (maximizing the security of the real worth of pensions and inflation fighting) first, is a contradiction in and of itself, and second, must, sooner or later, intensify the still dormant generation conflict into a civil war between the generations.

First, the index-like practice of projecting today's individual old-age income into the future (the so-called "dynamic pension"), which is already followed de facto and often dejure in many European welfare states (e.g. Sweden, the Federal Republic of Germany) cannot last forever. The constant worsening of the proportion of the aged, which can already be considered a sure thing up to the year 2000, will continually shrink the financial elbow-room of the public till. Unavoidably the government must resort to one or more of the following options: it must either cut back other programs (defense, education, infrastructure), raise the mandatory premiums for social insurance, or finance the inevitable social insurance deficit out of the general budget deficit. Since we can count on the last road to be the political path of least resistance, we can be sure that it will be followed, just as, for the most part, it has been up to this time.

The legal obligation to preserve dynamic real old-age income (an obligation which clearly exists in the Federal Republic of Germany) could lead to obligatory budget deficits with a tendency to increase from year to year. The tendency is designed to disguise politically the "hard" transfer of workers' incomes to the pockets of those no longer working. If so, the specific contribution of this sort of pension financing may not exactly be determinable, but its existence is demonstrable all the same. The income policy designed for the aged should avoid inflation in order to meet its self-imposed goals. Yet it stimulates the inflation process through its (quasi-monopolistic) non-adjustment of real pensions practically in the same way as the cost-push of firms and unions which dominate the market. In the meantime, senior citizen lobbies have organized themselves in the halls of social ministries of nearly all Western democracies. They represent their interest in the process of real non-adjustment much more effectively than do employee unions and so will probably strengthen the process of pension inflation in the future.

Second: The more explosive the disproportion between those under 60 still working and those over 60 no longer working threatens to become, the more openly must the governments of majority-rule democracies decide in favor of the "unproductive majority" as against the "productive minority." At the same time the dormant generation conflict, which up to this point has involved only young people disinterested in the state, will unavoidably evolve into an open generation conflict marked by rejection of the state. Since there is no indication that parties and politicians with government experience will let this process escalate, they will (in the absence of other politically applicable instruments) discover and learn to use corrective elements contained in the inflation rate itself.

Just as the former combination of the fear of inflation and the fear of losing jobs moderated, not to say "disciplined," the union wage-expansion policy, the progressive fear of the escalation of young worker and employee uprisings beginning in the factories and depressing the productivity rate will lead to a curbing of the pension dynamic with the help of the inflation rate long before the problem reaches its critical point.

The first indications of this trend have been visible in the Federal Republic of Germany since the slowdown in growth beginning in the early seventies. The initial characteristic step toward moderation was the abandonment of the business-cycle foundation of growth in pensions. Pensions, unlike wages represented purchasing power without a cost character. The second step was the explicit incorporation of the pension burden into the costs of the social state, which is becoming too expensive. The governing parties ventured a third step before the elections of 1976. After that date, the ruling coalition attempted to sugarcoat the decelerating climb in old-age pensions, while the opposition characterized this cautious correction of income distribution between the generations as misleading.

However the income balance between the generations is restored, whether through direct or indirect assaults, the general inflation rate will play an important, even stabilizing, role. This is so because the example of the old-age pension burden outlined briefly above repeats and confirms the two oldest experiences associated with an inflation which is both desired and, of course, controlled. First, it serves weak (incompetent, decentralized, democratic) governments as a noiseless, efficient instrument for the achievement of otherwise goals that are hard to reach. Second, inflation always contains a reward for risk, innovation and progress. Schumpeter's "process of creative destruction," the means by which "capitalism creates its structures and (after they have served their purpose) destroys them," always has been correlated with the concurrent inflation rate. To overlook this fact would be just as unreal as trying to present *Hamlet* without the Danish prince. Even Keynes asks himself the question in the 30th chapter of his still fascinating *Treatise on Money* of 1930 (as cited above), what would have come of the modern world formed by industrial capitalism if it only was able to fall back on the real savings of the 16th and 18th centuries? His answer: "The increase in wealth came wholly from increased activity, not diminished consumption."

V.

MONEY ILLUSION - IN WHOSE MIND?

5. MONEY ILLUSION - IN WHOSE MIND?

But what would happen if the whole world--entrepreneur, union member, pensioner, yes even the politician--all were to see through to the end results and redistribution effects which are associated with, if not actually caused by, inflation? What if no one nurtured "money illusions" any longer (the fondest wish of modern monetarists)?

Though one's first, not necessarily correct impression is that the question is terribly complex, it can be reduced to a relatively simple denominator. Naturally all entities, whether human or financial, committed to long-term money contracts, especially those which will be demanding payment in the future (owners of pecuniary assets, individual and collective savers, receivers of nominally fixed income and benefits) have their own thoughts about the future rate of inflation. They figure their thoughts into their claims as an extra component. And well they should. The very anticipation of a generally "expected rate of inflation" unfortunately leads to its self-fulfillment. This occurs all the more quickly and inexorably the more entrenched this way of protecting oneself against inflation becomes. For this reason it of course makes sense that the monetary officials (and not only they) have prohibited (up to this point with success) any "indexation" of credit positions and future income claims. The medicine would just worsen the sickness, not heal it. And the monetarist hope that if we all calculated solely in "real" terms, in the absence of inflation's profiteers we would also be rid of inflation (and hence also of inflation's "losers"), is just as realistic as the idea that without the discovery of swimming trunks, we'd all be nudists. We would simply find other fashions and materials for covering ourselves.

The plain and unpretentious truth is that the parliamentary nation-state, even if it possessed the proper insight into the nature of the inflation and adjustment cycle, cannot solve the world-wide inflation problem under "late industrial" conditions. The state's arsenal is literally too confined by the country's geographical borders, though no longer by economic and monetary borders. In the long run, competitive democracy and parliamentarism ruin only themselves with their stability policies designed just for domestic household use. They gamble away both their authority and their credibility if they wear themselves out professing radicalism of alternatives when their actual range of choices is one-dimensional and there are no genuine substantive options.

The failure of traditional Western anti-inflation policy therefore signifies a basic political-economic constitutional problem. Out of the disordered world economy there must emerge an ordered one. But what form must it take?

Inflation highlights the three weak spots this order must contend with: the currency, monopoly, and transfer problems. We can learn from the Western industrial countries, which had to realize at the beginning of this century that laissez-faire capitalism must place an "off limits" sign on the native, domestic areas of money, credit and market precedence. This they had to do if they wanted to preserve the blessings and advantages of a vital and efficient price mechanism for the whole system untainted by inflation and monopolistic price dictates. Likewise today each nation must repeat and expand this realization on a worldwide level for its own protection against inflation if not that of the others.

World inflation, however, has yet another, third dimension which is acquiring more and more significance and explosiveness: if we allow "only" financial transfer (indebtedness) to the developing countries as we have done up to the present, and deny them real transfer (liquidation of indebtedness through opening up markets and offering fair prices) will these nations follow OPEC's lead and use the manipulation of the terms of trade to recover that which has been withheld from them, thereby changing pricing politics to income politics?

The door to liberal reform of the world economic and currency order is still open. The crisis of the communist planned economies even gives this reform a unique chance of success in the present integrated world economy, helping to complete at the international level that which at the national level remains as a torso. After all, not even the strictest Manchester school advocates would maintain that the international "catch as catch can" system of multinational big banks and firms represents an ideal order. They too must be wary that a genuine collapse could grow out of "profit-inflation" quite soon. Fifty years after 1930 the preconditions of the great breakdown of the over-strained world economy are again existent: extreme discrepancies in balances of payments, oversized and nearly unpayable external debts, the blocking of both internal and external freedom of trade by national governments, and progressing depression.

Yet we also remember from the crisis of the '30s that the lethargy of the Great Depression was not broken by economic and monetary nationalism, but instead by the establishment of a new international order after the Second World War. As imperfect as the Bretton Woods System may have been, it was an approach to international money volume and liquidity control, to organized equalizations of balances of payments, to a debt process based on a policy of compulsory adjustment to fixed exchange rates. And it was a departure in development aid which had never before existed.

To this extent the fiasco of Western anti-inflation policies signifies more than just a mistaken diagnosis of inflation's causes and the most effective means of battling them. It also makes clear that in the one world economy where everyone depends on everyone else, no one can solve individual problems through isolation.

Instead, the solution will come only after the underlying distribution struggles are resolved through action on several fronts. Only if we succeed in channeling the stream of international liquidity which has flooded its banks, only if we effectively curtail the nearly unlimited upward freedom of movement of those prices dictated by international technological monopolies and raw material cartels, and only if we open reasonable paths for growth to the developing countries, through regulated indebtedness, will we be able to "control" the third and most dangerous of all distribution struggles.

This is not the struggle between the classes (which is approaching resolution) nor the struggle between the generations (which has become a community problem among the increasingly childless Western countries). Instead, it is the struggle between the rich and poor nations. When we control this conflict, and not before, we will also solve the problem of inflation.

FOOTNOTES - PART II

1. For a more detailed treatment by the author, see Goldne Zeiten führt ich ein - Caesar und sein Wirtschaftsimperium (Frankfurt, 1980), esp. ch. 7ff.

2. For an interesting treatment see Norbert Elias, Über den Prozess der Zivilisation, Soziogenetische und psychogenetische Untersuchungen (Bern and Munich, 1969). For a more comprehensive treatment of the seigniorage principle see W. Hankel, Weltwirtschaft - Vom Wohlstand der Nationen heute (Dusseldorf and Wien, 1977), pp. 239ff, and references cited therein.

3. See Bertrand Gill, "Bankwesen und Industrialisierung," in Europäische Wirtschaftsgeschichte, Vol. 3: Die industrielle Revolution, eds. C.M. Cipolla and K. Borchard, pp. 165ff.

4. Schumpeter in his Theorie der wirtschaftlichen Entwicklung (1911) and J.M. Keynes in the Tract on Monetary Reform (his treatment is rather incidental) discovered independently and almost simultaneously (as is so often the case in the history of economics) that redistribution is a function of taxation of monetary expansion and inflation. Keynes made an impressive test of his discovery in historic chapter 30 of his later work: Treatise on Money (1930).

5. See Paul Feyerabend, Wider den Methodenzwang, Skizze einer anarchistischen Erkenntnistheorie (Frankfurt, 1979), esp. the Foreword to the German edition, pp. 14ff. See also Fred Hirsch and John M. Goldthorpe, eds., The Political Economy of Inflation (Cambridge, 1978), Prologue, pp. 1ff.

6. See J.R. Hicks' brilliant essays, "The Two Triads, Lecture I-III," and "Monetary Theory and History - An Attempt at Perspective" in Critical Essays in Monetary Theory (Oxford, 1967), pp. 1-59 and 155-179.

7. C.S. Maier, "The Politics of Inflation in the Twentieth Century," in Hirsch and Goldthorpe, eds., op. cit., pp. 70f.

8. The author refines his xenomarket and OPEC analyses in "Wahrungsordnung bei weltweit ungeregelten kreditmärkten?" and in "OPEC: Öl oder Sand im Welt-Finanz-Getriebe? Ein Fall der Welt-Währungs- oder

Anlagenpolitik?" in *Gefährdete Weltfinanzen*, ed. H.-B. Schäfer (Bonn, 1980), pp. 21ff and 85ff.

9. Still the best survey of this controversy is a symposium sponsored by the American Enterprise Institute for Public Policy Research together with the U.S. Department of Treasury: *Eurocurrencies and the International Monetary System*, eds. Carl H. Stem, John H. Makin, and Dennis E. Logue (Washington, 1976).

10. See the earlier study by the present author together with F. Lehner, "Die gescheiterte Stabilitätspolitik und ihre politischen Folgen - Von der Unvereinbarkeit wirtschaftlicher Monopol - und demokratischer Konkurrenzsysteme," in *Hamburger Jahrbuch für Wirtschafts - und Gesellschaftspolitik*, Vol. 21 (1976).

11. See "Bericht eines Arbeitskreises der Gesellschaft für Sozialen Fortschritt," in *Sozialer Fortschritt*, Vol. 29, Nos. 7 and 8 (August 1980), pp. 145ff.

12. For a comparison, see A.F. Ehrbahr, "How to Save Social Security," *Fortune*, August 25, 1980, pp. 36ff.

13. The fact that the real costs of social insurance of an economy have nothing to do with the means of its financing was shown for the first time in German literature by Gerhard Mackenroth in his classic essay, "Die Reform der Sozialpolitik durch einen deutschen Sozialplan," in *Schriften des Vereins für Socialpolitik*, N.F., Vol. 4 (1952), pp. 61ff. In addition see by the present author, together with Gerhard Zweig, *Volkswirtschaftliche Grundfragen der Sozialreform* (*Siebzehn Punkte zur Sozialreform*) (Koln-Deutz, 1956), pp. 15ff, and Heinz A. Allekotte, *Möglichkeiten eines intertemporalen Belastungsausgleichs im Rahmen des Generationenvertrags der gesetzlichen Rentenversicherung*, a paper submitted at the 1980 annual meeting of the Verein fur Socialpolitik (Association of Social Policies) in Nürnberg (forthcoming). Also see the response of the federal government to the inquiry in *Grundprobleme der Bevölkerungsentwicklung in der Bundesrepublik Deutschland*, Bundestagsdrucksache 8/3299, 26 October 1979. For further treatment see "Berichtssystem Bildung - Beschäftigung, Ausgewählte Ergebnisse zur Situation der nachwachsenden Generation beim Übergang vom Bildungssystem in Beschäftigung" from

a press communiqué by the Bundesminister für Bildung und Wissenschaft (Federal Minister of Education and Science) (Bonn), 1 August 1980.

PART III

MODERN REACTIONS TO INFLATION: PRIVATE AND PUBLIC STRATEGIES

Robert A. Isaak

MODERN REACTIONS TO INFLATION: PRIVATE AND PUBLIC STRATEGIES*

Inflation is a social phenomenon: It is a public good that affects all human beings regardless of the nature of their private interests. The question of concern to most people is not, therefore, whether inflation is good or bad. Rather, the question is which management strategy is most effective in furthering particular life chances in a world where inflation is as inevitable as nasty weather. When storm clouds gather, the wise man does not curse at the sky but checks to see what kind of shape his umbrella is in. Part III focuses upon various inflation strategies which people, corporations and states have devised to protect themselves or to maximize their interests.

Three central questions will be considered:

(1) Which strategies have been used in the past decade in Western industrialization to protect against inflation or to benefit from it?

(2) How do these strategies interrelate?

(3) What are the likely consequences of these interrelationships for democracy and international society? Who stands to benefit most? Who least? And what are some of the long-term implications?

---

*The research behind this analysis was facilitated by grants from the U.S. Mission to the European Communities and the German Marshall Fund. The text benefitted from the perceptive suggestions of colleagues at the Johns Hopkins SAIS Bologna Center: economists Richard Pomfret, Ahmet Aker, Vera Zamagni, Stefano Zamagni, and particularly Wilhelm Hankel.

VI.

INDIVIDUAL COPING AND CHANGING LIFE CHANCES

> In Western civilization the idea of money exercises a great fascination--it is the fascination of an actual thing which has attained a metaphysical ideality or of a metaphysical entity which has attained actual existence. Spirits and ghosts are beings in such a middling state of existence; and money is both real and not real, like a spook. We invented money and we use it, yet we cannot either understand its laws or control its actions. It has a life of its own which it properly should not have ...
>
> --Lionel Trilling, *The Liberal Imagination*

VI. INDIVIDUAL COPING AND CHANGING LIFE CHANCES

"People always underestimate what's going to happen to them."

--Otto Eckstein

From the viewpoint of the individual, inflation implies the constant threat of the loss of value over time.[1] Paper money in one's pocket loses purchasing power against the prices of concrete goods one desires to buy. The interest rate from savings accounts does not keep up with the rate of inflation. Inflation has the effect of making material privation appear to be permanent, even in the richest Western societies. The theoretical "take-off" point at which the human being perceives total freedom from material needs and can self-actualize at a higher stage of development seems increasingly beyond grasp in the social environment of the late 20th century. Ours is a modern version of the classical Greek fate of Tantalus--reaching forever for a more refined level of consumption which increasing prices keep just beyond our means.

And even if one achieves a satiated level of material satisfaction, one discovers social deprivation in terms of status and position given the social scarcity that typifies modern industrial mass societies with keen competition for positional goods and facilities.[2] The "boot-strap theory of growth" as a surrogate for redistribution, according to which greater economic production by the whole society will pull up the poor at the bottom of the pile as well as the rich at the top has often proven to be illusory: under the best conditions, there is no guarantee that economic growth will not accentuate the distances between social groups, and in present circumstances the diminution of growth rates appears to make social polarization more important, not less. Inflation, in this context, often may serve as a smokescreen to cover social costs of mismanaged economic development, postponing the payment of the bill for popular redistribution programs of government through credit availability and currency devaluations. Everyone seems increasingly to have to run in place a little faster to keep up without any noticeable change in the relative distances between different classes of runners. Tempo is too often misconstrued as "progress." Indeed, time economists have demonstrated the tendency for greater affluence to make modern man more harried rather than less.[3] Time becomes scarcer as the output of material goods increases while the time in which to use them remains constant. Two consequences result that inflation serves only to intensify: the individual needs additional time for consumption and additional income to maintain his or her position in society.[4]

In advanced industrial societies, time-frames distort individual perceptions of life chances. Whereas earlier in the century sociologist Max Weber used the concept of "life chances" to imply a competitive struggle for survival among individuals or types of people, as the century comes to a close sociologists such as Ralf Dahrendorf interpret "life chances" as the odds of fulfilling the full range of human possibilities given the individual's social ties and options.[5] But both of these viewpoints are distorted by the time and social perspective of the observer. Perhaps overinfluenced by Darwin and Social Darwinism, Weber put more emphasis upon survival than was appropriate for the situation he was describing. And by the same token, apparently Dahrendorf took the social promise in the abnormally high growth rates of the 1950s and 1960s too much to heart, underestimating the costs and preconditions for the satisfaction of lower level material needs.[6] However, Dahrendorf's recently diminished high expectations are typical of our era and are not unrelated to our social tolerance of high rates of inflation in advanced industrial societies.[7] For since the Great Depression, these societies have been cushioned at the bottom of their economic cycles against the risk of repeating the 1930s, allowing people to take survival for granted and to lift their sights to ever higher levels of material consumption and human fulfillment. To ask people so socialized to suddenly cap the top of the economic cycle to control inflation and to lower their expectations accordingly is a bit more than one can expect, particularly in popularly elected democracies where politicians must promise prosperity, not austerity, to keep their jobs.

Nevertheless, the decade of the 1970s did serve to unsettle the expectations of many people in advanced industrial societies, if not to lower them. The OPEC oil price hikes and unpredictability of government policy in the United States, not to mention the unstable world situation, increased mass perceptions of uncertainty concerning the future. For example, almost half of the 1,873 Americans interviewed nationwide by the Washington Post in April 1980 expressed the fear that within the coming year they would be worse off financially, a rate double that found in a November 1979 survey. Inflation was the most important personal concern of many of those interviewed, who reported they were cutting down on gasoline consumption, taking extra jobs, borrowing to pay bills and looking for ways to cut expenses.[8] Later, a 1980 Gallup Poll confirmed that inflation was the central American issue.

The basic logic of individuals in advanced, mixed economies such as those of Western Europe and the United States stems from the ideology or myth of private self-sufficiency: Each person has the right and duty to maximize his or her own private and family interests (and to cut down private costs). To the extent one can get the state or someone else to pick up the bill for life expenses, so much the better. In Europe the subsidies for the welfare and medical care of the old have progressed to the point where some even buy tea on the state from the pharmacy, while in the United States although state subsidies for senior citizens are growing, they are not necessarily comfortable, perhaps making Americans more future-oriented in their "security strategies" before they retire than are many Europeans. Nevertheless, a 1977 comparison of social security benefits in ten industrial nations (including the U.S., eight European countries and Canada) established that a middle-income couple, where both partners are 65 or older, can expect to receive retirement benefits of not less than 45% of the last gross earnings from covered employment, or 60% of the last net earnings, allowing them to maintain approximately the same living standard they had enjoyed before retirement.[9] But if double-digit inflation rates should once again come to plague Western industrial democracies, this projection may well prove to be optimistic and many retired middle-class people could suffer from a significant lowering of their standard of living. Experts generally agree that to permit all but the highest income workers to maintain preretirement standards of living requires 60-80% of gross retirement income, given shifts that occur in tax liabilities, living expenses, and consumption and savings patterns in retirement.[10]

Inflation serves to stimulate the Western logic of maximizing individual interest while simultaneously undermining the collective conditions that make individual self-sufficiency possible. As prices escalate faster, as income increases, the individual's financial position becomes increasingly uncertain. The percentage of American employees covered by cost-of-living escalators rose from 26% in 1965 to 58% in 1980. But such cost-of-living clauses usually cover only 50% to 70% of consumer price increases.[11] And few U.S. pension or retirement agreements are indexed for cost-of-living increases, which becomes increasingly significant as medical science extends the age of life expectancy. The American Census Bureau projects that of the population 65 years old and over between 1980 and the year 2000 the percentage of people in the 65-74 age bracket will decline from 54.5% to 45.4%, whereas those in the 75-84 bracket will increase from 37.1% to 44.1% and those in the age 85 and over bracket will increase from 8.4% to 10.5%.[12] So most American workers are locked into a social situation in which they must worry annually about how much inflation is reducing the real value of their wages and must worry even more about inflation's effect upon fixed-dollar private pension benefits. Curiously, bad publicity has made Americans distrustful about the reliability of Social Security benefits providing full cost-of-living adjustments in the 1970s, whereas they seem to view their private pension plans as basically secure, although these are usually not indexed and the American government appears to be overloaded with pressures to keep many of the private pension plans afloat.[13] But no matter how the vulnerability is sliced, the individual is generally correct in perceiving that inflation is undermining his bargaining power to cope with everyday expenses, not to mention his long-term financial security.

Individual strategies aimed at coping with inflationary change are often eclectic and complex. Nevertheless, it is possible to identify several typical patterns (what sociologist Max Weber would have called "ideal types" of inflation strategies), which individuals seem to draw upon to create their own strategic or portfolio mix. Initially, of course, one must distinguish between those who have merely _reactions_ rather than _strategies_, that is, between those who respond in an almost unconscious impulsive manner to inflationary change and those who have consciously conceived future-oriented game plans to cope with what happens to them. In his book _Loss and Change_, sociologist Peter Marris demonstrates that when individuals undergo severe loss or extreme change in their lives they respond to a conservative impulse by attempting to recover stability through old values and patterns. Perhaps the overwhelming majority of people in the whirlwind of change of the late 20th century suffer from "the conservative impulse." Still, it is possible to distinguish those who merely react defensively through a conservative impulse to hang on to what they have from those who transcend defensive reactions to create more positive strategies that require them to take some risks for the future.

In categorizing possible individual inflation strategies from the most defensive to the most aggressive and from the least future-oriented to the most future-oriented, one can identify at least four "ideal types:" The Defeatist, The Free Rider, The Maintenance Man and The Entrepreneur. Each of these four "pure" types of individual inflation strategy can be compared in terms of risk orientation, time orientation, guiding motive, consumption pattern and characteristic portfolio mix (as shown in Figure VI-1).[14]

The Defeatist takes as few risks as possible, preferring to cut costs rather than to risk assets in an uncertain environment. In terms of time orientation, the Defeatist is past-oriented, perhaps thinking back to the economic chaos of the 1930s and believing that another Great Depression is just around the corner. The guiding motive of this type is passive or defensive, quivering with the fear of loss--Marris's "conservative impulse" ad absurdum. As a consumer, the Defeatist is conservative--a bargain-hunter and belt-tightener. The Defeatist's portfolio mix has a security focus featuring an insured savings account, perhaps a six-month savings certificate and a few government bonds, and maybe a small family house that will be kept indefinitely (and certainly until the mortgage is totally paid off). Job changes or career shifts are unthinkable for the Defeatist until it is too late and necessity demands change for survival.

The Free Rider, in contrast, enjoys taking high risks at no cost or at low cost, specializing in living on someone else's bill. Present-oriented, the Free Rider fondly thinks of extending the 1960s when economic growth was often taken for granted and social benefits for the individual seemed to become a matter of right and entitlement, rather than of duty or reward

Figure VI-1

IDEAL TYPES OF INDIVIDUAL INFLATION STRATEGIES	Risk Orientation	Time Orientation	Guiding Motive	Consumption Pattern	Characteristic Portfolio Mix
The Defeatist	As few risks as possible: cut costs rather than risk assets in uncertain environment	Past-oriented (thinks of 1930s)	Passive or defensive: fear of loss	Conservative: the bargain-hunter and belt-tightener	Security focus: insured savings accounts and six-month certificates plus a few government bonds
The Free Rider	High risk at no or low cost	Present-oriented (thinks of 1960s)	Active-passive: maximin -- maximize gains and minimize costs	Mixed but consistent: high consumption when others pay, low otherwise	Cheap money (debt) focus: credit cards, exploit government welfare, unemployment and lending programs, foundation grants, philanthropists and rich friends
The Maintenance Man	Limited risks at moderate cost to keep up with the game	Present-oriented (thinks of 1980s)	Passive-active: coopt change to maintain stability	Liberal: consume more now before costs go even higher	Stable-return and liquidity focus: short-term money-market shares, buys single family home and vacation home, select blue-chip stocks, perhaps also modern art and stamps. Treasury bills when at advantageous interest rate. Little cash in bank.
The Entrepreneur	High risks even at high cost to beat the game	Future-oriented (thinks of the coming decade)	Hyper-active or aggressive: invests all energy and resources in the highest likely future pay-off	Mixed and erratic: all or nothing	Highest-return focus: gambles on business cycle -- stocks, bonds, commodities, gold, real estate, speculation, opens small businesses, etc.

for effort. The guiding motive of the Free Rider is an active-passive one: maximin--maximizing individual gains and minimizing personal costs. This type is a game theorist's dream of a rational, self-interested player, always looking for a comfortable saddle-point and the ultimate short-cut. The Free Rider's consumption pattern is mixed but consistent: high consumption when others pay, low otherwise. The characteristic Free Rider portfolio mix is focused on cheap money or debt at low interest rates: utilizing credit cards and exploiting government welfare and social programs, unemployment and lending programs, foundation grants, philanthropists and rich friends. Highest pay and fringe benefit for least time at work constitute the criteria for the Free Rider's ultimate job. The dream vacation would be to have someone else pitch a tent for the Free Rider on a deserted beach at St. Tropez, preferably with a voluptuous sleeping mate.

The Maintenance Man takes limited risks at moderate cost to keep up with the financial game and business cycle, to keep even with inflation. This present-oriented, realist thinks short-term into the 1980s, guided by a passive-active motive: to coopt change in order to insure stability. As far as consumption goes, the Maintenance Man is a liberal and hedonist, consuming more of quality now before costs go even higher. The characteristic portfolio mix of the Maintenance Man makes this the ultimate managerial strategy: the focus is upon stable returns and liquidity with enough flexibility to adapt to the business cycle. Rather than overusing local banks, the Maintenance Man uses a national or international financial service to open a money-market-fund account, buys a series of single-family homes (bargaining up in value and tax and mortgage advantages) and a rentable vacation home, selects blue-chip stocks, or more likely, stamps and modern art originals, and plays conservatively with stocks and bonds, leaving little cash to atrophy against inflation in the savings bank. A cool-headed manager who seeks constantly to open up new options without risking the foundation of past gains, the Maintenance Man keeps a diverse portfolio, is flexible in terms of job or career shifts or relocating, and functions like a well-serviced, skillfully driven, up-to-date automobile that seeks out superhighways and carefully pre-targeted motels, restaurants and diversions on the way to Progress.

Compared to the Maintenance Man, the Entrepreneur is the gambler who takes high risks even at high costs in an end-run attempt to come out ahead of inflation, to beat the financial game. The entrepreneur takes "the conservative impulse" and runs with it imaginatively, hoping to outwit uncertainty with at least one overwhelming success. Marris argues that acute sense of loss, change and status deprivation provide the impulse for innovative entrepreneurship, which depends upon a delicate balance of handicap and potential advantage. The Entrepreneur seeks to change the world in order to avoid changing himself, displacing into original enterprises the goals learned from society that cannot be satisfied within that society's orthodox framework.[15] Unusually sensitive to how inflation is demoting his or her life chances in the hierarchy of modern society, the Entrepreneur grows tired of waiting in line or of serving in a bureaucratic seniority system and seeks to skip steps up the ladder through brilliant, innovative behavior. Future-oriented, often to the point of thinking a decade or two ahead, the Entrepreneur's guiding motive is hyperactive or aggressive--the thrust to invest all energy and resources in the direction of the highest likely pay-off. Typically, the Entrepreneur's consumption pattern is all or nothing, prince or pauper. The characteristic portfolio mix of this type of strategy is focused upon the highest return, astute gambles on the business cycle, swinging in and out of commodities, stocks, bonds, gold, real estate, and the founding of small or big businesses. Ultimately, the Entrepreneur is a financial romantic who well understands the meaning of Goethe's words: "_Himmelhochjauchend zu Tode betruebt_" ("from the highest exultation to deepest depression").

As "ideal types" or the theoretical extremes of typical patterns of behavior, it may well be that few actual human beings consistently live up to the description of The Defeatist, The Free Rider, The Maintenance Man, or The Entrepreneur. Most people have mixed strategies, drawing inspirations from each of these types at various times in their lives, but nevertheless allowing one or two of the types to preoccupy them. In terms of the individual's ability to cope most effectively with inflation in the future, the most relevant question is, perhaps, what was the optimum mix of these strategy types in the recent past (the 1970s) that is apt to be still relevant in the present decade. Or, more concretely, which combination of portfolio investments has proven to be most successful? Under what conditions?

Consider first that large number of people who did not consciously invest at all in the 1970s, passive Defeatists, if you will, who merely lived with inflation. Although psychologically many of this group had a sense of being increasingly impoverished by inflation, particularly given the television media's distorting symbolic focus on what happened to the cost of a "market basket" of food in the past year, American statistics indicate that the costs of inflation were actually less than supposed. Real incomes (after inflation and tax have been discounted) rose at almost the same rate during the inflationary years of 1972-1978 as during the boom years 1966-1972.[16] And when the curve of real per capita income did turn down in 1979, it seemed to have been due to government attempts to slow inflation by halting economic growth. The relative disadvantage of the poor, the blacks and the aged did not appear to become worse in this period, despite popular beliefs to the contrary. As economist Robert Heilbroner noted, "The distribution of the population on the steps of the national escalator ... remained about the same, although the escalator itself has been moving faster."[17]

Among the Defeatists were not a few who instinctively saved until they could afford a downpayment on a single-family home, a mini-fortress to protect their privatism from the storm of inflationary change. This half-conscious, "natural" purchase often ends up being the best investment people make in their lives. As an illustration, within the United States a dollar invested in a house in 1968 rose to $1.29 in purchasing power in 1978. If the same dollar was kept in the owner's pocket it would have fallen to $.53; if invested in a common stock it would have been worth $.78; if held in a savings account worth $.89; and if put in a corporate bond, up to $1.20--still less than housing appreciation.[18] And between 1978 and 1980, American housing prices shot up at an even higher rate until the moderation and decline of 1981-82. This data makes it possible to distinguish between the Vested and Uninvested or Disinvested Defeatist strategies. The Vested Defeatist is one who owns a private house or apartment that more than keeps up with the inflation rate, but whose other money is apt to go down the drain (in a relative sense) either under the mattress (falling to $.53 on the dollar) or in a savings account ($.89 on the dollar). However the Uninvested or Disinvested Defeatist who does not own a private residence (whether due to lack of funds, to a disinclination to invest or to foolish divestment) is much worse off. For example, a Vested Defeatist who bought a house in 1979 for $63,000 (the average U.S. price that year), would be financially ahead of a renting Disinvested Defeatist after 14 months, assuming that the renter receives an 8% yield on an alternative investment and that the buyer pays 10 percent down with a 12 percent mortgage (and including closing costs).[19] In sum, the single most important financial distinction between individuals in coping with inflation in the 1970s may well have been between those who owned a house at the beginning of this inflationary decade and those who did not.

For the Vested Defeatists, the inflationary 1970s were more often than not an unexpected bonanza in terms of their increases in real estate value and the resulting stabilization of their life chances. Many, if not most, did not foresee the extent of the inflation and merely went happily along for the ride (hanging on tight). Their conservative impulse just happened to be correctly targeted for the economic cycle that came. Chance, as Aristotle put it, is the arrow that strikes the fellow standing next to you (the Disinvested Defeatist in this case).

The group hit hardest by the inflationary waves of the 1970s were those retired on fixed incomes--particularly in the United States.[20] If not Vested or Disinvested Defeatists, many of the smaller group of "private" pensioneers were forced to become Free Riders by default: Managers of institutionalized pension plans invested much of their shares (without their "vote" and often without their awareness) into stocks that failed to keep up in value with inflation. Indeed, American stocks averaged a return of less than 3% through the decade of the 1970s.[21] And someone investing in America's factories, mines, transport systems, patents, and everything but its farms and financial institutions in a systematic, average way between 1964 and 1973 would have seen the after-tax return on his investment decline some 40 percent.[22] Individuals do learn from negative pay-offs, and at least 7 million shareholders defected from the stock market in the 1970s, mainly young investors and smart money managers, leaving equities to the giant institutional investors often representing the old and retired. For example, between 1970 and 1975, the number of investors in stocks dropped in every age group but that of individuals 65 and older, whereas the number of investors in this older group went up by more than 30%.[23] Either the elderly did not understand the rapid changes in the financial market or, more likely, they were fixed in situations where they were unable to adapt to these changes and they continued to cling to stocks. No doubt government pressures on giant private pension funds to prop up the stock market (not to mention legal restrictions) played a role in this cruel mismanagement of the pension shares of older people unable to defend themselves and too passive to speak out in protest.[24] The new flexibility in the Labor Department regulations (under the Employee Retirement Income Security Act of 1974) that went into effect on July 23, 1979 is a hopeful step in the right direction, allowing pension fund money to go not only into listed stocks and high-quality bonds but into shares of little companies, real estate, gold, diamonds and commodity futures. Although this government shift could undermine the stock market, the 1982 U.S. stock recovery and government Individual Retirement Account legislation may serve to counteract this possibility. Yet, as Robert S. Salomon Jr. of Salomon Brothers suggests: "We are running the risk of immobilizing a substantial portion of the world's wealth in someone's stamp collection."[25]

People are coming to realize to what extent inflation has eroded the private pension system. Since American living costs rose at an annual rate of 7.4% throughout the 1970s, the purchasing power of an individual who retired in 1970 was cut by more than 50% (assuming the company did not provide any interim increases). In another five years, at the same rate of inflation, such a pension would only be worth a third of its original value. The inflation rate in the United States in 1979 was over 13%. At an inflation rate of 12%, a fixed pension will lose 66% of its value in ten years and 90% of its value in twenty years.[26] Should double-digit inflations return in the late 1980s or thereafter, these pension erosion figures may become painfully real.

The decline in the value of equities during the 1970s gives a hollow ring to management consultant

Peter Drucker's claim that the United States is moving fast towards "pension fund socialism." As of 1974 about 30 percent of the stock market had been purchased by institutional investors for employee pension funds. This trend leads Drucker to argue that the means of production of the American economy are being run for the benefit of the country's employees and that this new kind of socialism will lead to a class struggle between pensioned employees desiring to maximize corporate earnings and younger, currently employed workers who want to increase their incomes regardless of effects on earnings per share. By the late 1980s Drucker projects that the American population will have become so old demographically that pension funds will no longer produce surpluses to be invested in the national economy but will have to pay out more than they can take in from those still working. This capital shortage, in turn, will threaten the very existence of the new rentier class created by these pension funds. Perhaps the most important observation which Drucker makes, however, is that pension fund employees are at a great disadvantage compared to other investors who can buy and sell securities independently since they cannot act rationally in their own interest.[27] The pensioneers are at the mercy of their fund managers, in whom one cannot have the greatest confidence given their overinvestment in a declining stock market in the first place. As individual interest becomes institutionalized, as the investment decision-making power is separated from those in whose interests it is executed, mediocre Maintenance Man strategies are employed to preserve stability over everything else--including profitability. Or, as economist Mancur Olson has put it more generally, voluntary collective action cannot be counted on to maximize an individual group member's interests, and the larger the group the less the likelihood that the individual's interests will be maximized.[28]

Where, then, can the individual turn who already has a house and who has rationally concluded he cannot trust his pension fund to provide enough to secure his standard of living in retirement? Where should he invest and what strategy should he follow?

The simple answer in an inflationary era is to diversify investment in hard assets, a balance between the Maintenance Man and Entrepreneur strategies aimed at the concrete. During the 1970s, for example, stamps appreciated more consistently than almost anything else including gold, which came in a close second due to speculative swings in the buying and selling of this commodity. Diamonds and farmland ranked as steady gainers in the next category, followed by single-family houses. Significantly behind all these tangible assets came average appreciation through investment in foreign currencies and high-grade corporate bonds which more or less kept even with the rise in the Consumer Price Index (the most popular indicator of the inflation rate, despite its problems).[29] Stocks, of course, trailed the CPI.

Art works constitute another fruitful category of hard assets, which often outpaced the stock market in the past decade and in not a few cases the inflation rate as well. A 1980 study by the Economist Intelligence Unit of London compared the price records of 182 art works (in fourteen different categories that have been sold at least twice in an auction in the last twenty years) with the Dow Jones industrial index. Despite the limits of the sample, the broad conclusions of the study have not been challenged: The prices of modern paintings, books and prints did a great deal better than equivalent stock market investments would have reaped. In the second category in terms of percent of appreciation were furniture, antique silver, Chinese ceramics and English 18th and 19th century paintings. And although American, Impressionist and Old Master paintings generally paid off, they often did less well than average. The criteria which determine the value of art works in each category (more or less in order of priority) are quality, condition, rarity, fashion and beauty (or sex appeal).[30] In 1980 record auction prices were reached in not a few categories: Vincent Van Gogh's "Le Jardin du Poete, Arles" sold for $5.2 million, J.M.W. Turner's "Juliet and Her Nurse" for $6.4 million and Pablo Picasso's "Saltimbanque With Arms Crossed" for $14.8 million.

A more flexible and liquid investment than hard assets (popular in the late 1970s because of rising interest rates in the United States) is to buy shares in a money market, one of the most profitable off-springs of mutual funds. By constantly rolling over short-term paper investments in relatively secure sectors, such as Treasury Bills and municipal bonds, money-fund managers have outpaced the returns on stocks and bonds by a considerable amount for their clients. But as interest rates fall, the astute Maintenance-Entrepreneur shifts his investment with the business cycle--perhaps into bonds where prices rise with a decline in long-term interest rates. As stock prices fall after short-term interest rates have peaked, perhaps indicating the beginning of a recession, the optimum strategist waits three or four months for them to bottom out and then buys energy-related, high technology or inflation-proof stocks (like beer and tobacco) as they start to move upward. The secret of success in playing the business cycle in stocks and bonds is knowing when to get out of them, often signaled by a rise in short-term interest rates and after having held them for 18 months or so, according to Irwin L. Kellner, senior vice-president and chief economist of Manufacturers Hanover Trust Co., the fourth largest American bank. Kellner maintains that these interest-rate led recession and recovery cycles are inevitable and can be used as the basis of profitable financial planning: rising short-term interest rates signal an increase in inflation, raising bond rates, attracting money from the stock market, which in turn causes a decline in stock prices. At this point the Maintenance-Entrepreneur has already reinvested again in the liquid money market funds and is waiting for the next recession.[31] The cyclic investment in bonds is based on the assumption that inflation is moderating; at that point when inflation begins to accelerate, it is important to disinvest from bonds quickly. Figure VI-2 illustrates one strategic viewpoint of how the optimum manager could cope with the recession cycle that began in 1980.[32]

Even those in a position to afford to practice this optimum managerial strategy, however, find they have a hard time keeping up given the new information they must constantly process, the operational details involved in switching funds around and their regular job, family and leisure activities. More than half the families in the United States, for example, can hardly afford the prerequisites for this optimum strategy: their annual income in 1980 was below the $20,517 the Department of Labor estimates would be required for an American family of four to maintain in a moderate standard of living in a metropolitan area.[33] It is not just everyone who could spend a record $31,000 for an 1822 bottle of _Chateau Lafite_

Figure VI-2

WHERE TO PUT YOUR MONEY.....

	...as recession deepens	... as the economy recovers			
Stocks	Money-center banks, Insurance, and other Interest-sensitive groups	Tobacco, drugs high-technology and other blue-chip stocks	Machinery and other cyclical industries	Energy, natural resources, commodity, and other inflation-sensitive groups	
Fixed-income	Money-market instruments, including commercial paper Treasury bills	Intermediate and long-term bonds		Six-month bills and Certificates of Deposit	
Commodity futures	Treasury bills and other interest-rate futures	Lumber and plywood	Gold	Industrial Commodities and metals	Meat and other foods
Real estate and syndications	Office buildings in growth areas	Individual condominiums in resort areas and townhouses in good residential areas		Shopping centers	
Art and collectibles	18th century English furniture, Art Deco objects, American studio pottery, and other undervalued categories	Tiffany lamps, 19th century European paintings, and other heavily bought fad categories			

at a 1980 wine auction, as did restaurant owner John Grisanti in San Francisco.

Individual reactions to inflation in the 1970s can be summarized as follows: (1) Inflationary periods stimulate individuals to maximize their interests but undermine the conditions that make it possible; (2) Inflation appears to intensify conflict between classes and social groups without fundamentally changing the social distance between them--everyone is forced to run faster on the same escalator; (3) The payoffs of the 1970s rewarded those who invested in real estate and hard assets and punished those who invested in stocks; (4) The group most punished by investment in stocks were the elderly over 65; (5) The groups whose life chances were most negatively affected by this inflationary period were the unemployed, those too poor or foolish to invest in a house and the old--people forced into the Free Rider strategy by default; (6) The social effect of the inflation of the 1970s was to make material need satisfaction appear insatiable, to stimulate perceptions of status deprivation and to speed up the tempo of social life without increasing opportunities or real affluence; and (7) Although a flexible balance between the Maintenance Man and Entrepreneur strategies may be optimum for an individual seeking to cope with inflation, the majority of people are not in a position to afford the prerequisites for this strategy mix and often make do with some combination of Defeatist and Free Rider strategies.

VII.

CORPORATE AND INSTITUTIONAL STRATEGIES

VII. CORPORATE AND INSTITUTIONAL STRATEGIES

> "Today's chief executives don't have the menu to determine what their options are. They have to go out and search for the menu."
>
> --Herbert A. Simon

As one moves from individual to group strategies in coping with inflation, a diffusion of motives, responsibility and institutional costs diminish the odds of optimality. As economist Mancur Olson put it, "unless the number of individuals in a group is quite small, or unless there is coercion or some other special device to make individuals act in their common interest, rational, self-interested individuals will not act to achieve their common or group interests.[34] When the individual has to carry all the responsibilities and potential costs alone, that is one thing. But when there is a large, anonymous group, the individual member is often overwhelmed by the temptation to become a Free Rider and to settle for mediocre group compromises in which investment decisions are less often rationally targeted for high gains than they are spread out to reduce risks in order to keep things going as they are.[35] There is in human organizations, in short, a conservative bias that consistently favors the Maintenance Man and discourages the Entrepreneur. And inflation often appears to reinforce this conservative bias in large organizations.

Of course the carrot (the promise of being promoted) and the stick (the threat of being fired) mitigate against this bias somewhat. But in the Pavlovian uncertainty that comes from the mixed signals one receives in working bureaucracies, most human beings with common sense settle for the security promised by the Maintenance strategy of being a team-player and do not risk rocking the boat. Such motivations lead people into what psychologist Irving Janis has termed "group think"--a rigid social tendency to go along with the viewpoint of the majority of the elite, keeping doubts to oneself. No wonder that the concern over creating a viable corporate strategy has become such a high priority among business people. The top dog surrounded by yes-men often finds that the rapidly changing environment leaves him out in the cold without any warning, and the organization and his successors suddenly find themselves in desperate need of a new game plan.

The shift from more predictable, generally stable growth rates of the 1950s and 1960s to the inflationary uncertainties and sharp recessionary drops of the 1970s and 1980s called for a change in types of corporate strategy to meet the new environmental challenges. Fred Gluck, chairman of McKinsey and Company's strategic management steering committee, maintains that the goal of planning in the present era is to shift thinking "away from methodology and toward clver, creative, insightful, and opportunistic decision-making to gain a competitive edge; people understand a whole lot more about business strategy than they do about corporate strategy."[36] The inflationary environment, in short, calls for a redirection of corporate strategy from mere Maintenance thinking to Entrepreneurial thinking. Figure VII-1 illustrates the time perspective, risk orientation and concrete strategies or objectives involved in such a management shift.

Many chief executives of corporations today were brought up in an era that emphasized caution over entrepreneurship, that stressed the Maintenance caretaker objectives of short-term profit growth, good price-earning ratios and a stable return on investments or assets.[37] "In a very real sense, the role of the chief executive as entrepreneur is being replaced by his role as ringmaster, while the line manager's traditional role of implementor and conservator is being reversed to that of entrepreneur."[38] The time perspective of the Maintenance strategy is short-term to medium-range, aiming either for quick profit turnover or to assure an increasing market share for mature products. The Maintenance manager has a limited risk orientation and focuses upon cutting costs and maximizing benefits within the organization. As William C. Norris, founder, chairman and chief executive officer of Control Data Corporation notes: "Today's emphasis is on immediate payoffs from marginal improvement in existing offerings and from lower labor costs through mechanization and automation. In such an environment, it is no surprise that development of new products and services takes a back seat. But big business is not alone. It shares its apathetic, risk-avoiding, selfish, and reactionary profile with other sectors, including academia, organized labor, private foundations, the churches and government."[39] The

Figure VII-1

IDEAL TYPES OF CORPORATE STRATEGIES IN INFLATIONARY PERIODS	Time Perspective	Risk Orientation	Concrete Strategies and Objectives
Maintenance	Stable short-term profit turn-over Medium-range investments to assure increase in market share of mature, profitable products	Low-risk orientation (focus upon cutting costs and maximizing benefits within firm)	-Maximize short-term profits -Avoid areas of vulnerability -Reorganize business units within firm, targeting for specific markets -Consolidate company's financial position by buying back own stocks, even with loans -Develop more specific inflation indicators than CPI -Shorten reaction time within business units through use of limited computer models -Diversification within firm to cover risks and follow shifting markets -Mergers with large companies in similar fields -Mechanize and automate to cut labor costs
Entrepreneurial	Long-term planning and investment in new areas of greatest potential growth	High-risk orientation (focus upon maximizing benefits or cutting costs by investing outside firm nationally or internationally)	-Acquisition of smaller companies to reduce resource dependence or to increase innovation and technology -Bring in outside consultants and scientists to strengthen long-term financial planning and research and development (R&D) -Increase R & D budget -Increase individual pay-offs within company for those who creatively and successfully take short-term risks for high long-term gains -Lobby in government to cut costs due to environmental regulation and to seek tax subsidies to encourage long-term capital formation, R & D, etc. -Foreign expansion to follow customers, match competition, lower labor costs, lower resource dependency, increase world market share and counter international currency and tax fluctuations

popularity of risk-avoidance in modern society recalls the prediction of economist Joseph Schumpeter that at advanced stages of development the capitalist economy undermines the vital entrepreneurial or innovative function as technological progress and the bureaucratic administration of large corporations transform innovation itself into a routine matter and as committees and teams of experts are substituted for individual initiative.[40]

Accordingly, one of the corporate strategies of Maintenance managers is to change the mix of businesses to avoid areas of vulnerability, as when the policymakers of Esmark Inc. decided in 1978 to shift their Swift and Company fresh meat division from a commodity business to a consumer product company to avoid factors beyond their control. This change meant divesting $400 million in commodity businesses (like soybean milling) and investing $670 million to acquire new consumer product lines (like International Playtex Company) within the next five years. Another Maintenance strategy is to reorganize business units within the organization to adapt more rapidly to changing markets, shortening reaction time within the units through the use of carefully targeted computer models. Managers at R.J. Reynolds Industries Inc. used this strategy in the 1970s to compile information from the corporation's six operating units and to project cash flows instantaneously (and the shortfalls any division might have and their effect on the company's over-all growth targets). Public Service Electric and Gas Company of New Jersey uses a similar strategy to monitor its energy requirements, equipment use and price fluctuations. A closely related strategy is for companies and large institutions to develop more accurate inflation indicators of inflation than the Consumer Price Index (CPI), which tended to overstate inflation in the 1970s because of its heavy weighting towards housing and mortgage markets.[41] General Electric Company even initiated a companywide program to train upper management to adjust costs and income for inflation.

In contrast to these mere Maintenance strategies, Entrepreneurial strategies stress long-term planning and investment in the areas of greatest potential growth, and have a high-risk orientation, focusing on maximizing benefits or cutting costs through activities <u>outside</u> the corporation. Entrepreneurship transcends security concerns and aims for extraordinary gains through extraordinary innovation or risk. One successful entrepreneurial coup can set a whole population of Maintenance managers scurrying to catch up, often much too late to reap the first few years of harvest. Thus, in 1978 the Entrepreneurs of Union Carbide Corporation shocked the Maintenance men of Gulf Oil Corporation by announcing that they had developed a new process to make low-density polyethylene at a cost of 20% less than Gulf's conventional process. Gulf had counted on gaining and holding the Number 2 position in the market for low-density polyethylene film as part of a five-year corporate strategy. But the researchers in the chemical division made a critical false assumption biased by Maintenance thinking: that technological breakthroughs in polyethylene manufacture were improbable and spending for research and development could be kept minimal. The Entrepreneurs of Union Carbide left Gulf with an uncomfortable choice of either licensing the new technology from their competitors at an extremely steep price or belatedly shifting funds from other corporate targets to intensify research and development in order to discover a process to match their rival. The Gulf managers choose the latter alternative. But if they are unable to come through with a technological breakthrough before their plant capacity must be expanded they may have to leave the business. If so, their decision to abort may be just as belated (and costly) as was their decision to step up research and development. In a rapidly changing environment stoked by inflation the penalty for not having a creative Entrepreneurial strategy can be staggering. The failure of the Chrysler Corporation and Ford Motor Company to develop a small, low-gas-consumption car in time to match the competition of innovative Japanese and European automobile manufacturers is another case in point.

The failure to put enough energy and funding into Entrepreneurial strategies in the 1970s left Chrysler and Ford in a weak position when the recession arrived in 1980. Chrysler had to reduce its spending plans by $136 million for 1980 and Ford Motor Company planned to cut $2.5 billion from its domestic capital spending budget between 1980 and 1985. Maintenance thinking thus became a negative, self-fulfilling prophecy, a desperate running in place just to keep up. General Motors, in contrast, whose Entrepreneurs had developed a successful small car on time to compete with foreign competition was in a position to increase its spending between 1980 and 1985 by $2 billion, to a record $40 billion.[42] Still, even General Motors looked like a poor performer when compared with the percentage increase of sales for 1978-1979 of major European and Japanese auto firms. During this year General Motors sales increased 5% (Ford Motor, 2%, Chrysler -27%), compared to Volkswagen's 15%, Daimler-Benz's 13%, Peugeot-Citroen's 10%, Toyota's 11%, and Honda Motor's 16%.[43] Moreover, inflation inflates the profit figures of major companies making them appear to be doing better than they actually are. For example, if the 1980 total assets of General Motors are listed according to the traditional basis of historical cost, they come to $19 billion with an apparent 15% after-tax return annually. But if one uses instead the value of the $50 billion required to replace these same assets--the real value if inflation is discounted--they yielded an annual return of only 6%.[44]

Entrepreneurial inflation-protection strategies are, of course, just as important for non-business institutions as they are for corporations, if not more so. For example, unlike American pension funds, European institutions have been investing up to 40% of their money in hard assets for a long time, particularly in real estate.[45] The British Rail Superannuation Pension Fund spent $58 million in fine arts in 1974, buying up everything from Picasso's Young Man in Blue to 12th century candlesticks. But some American institutional investors have apparently learned from watching. For example, the Minneapolis Teachers Retirement Fund Association has invested in fast-food stores such as Burger King and Kentucky Fried Chicken, which are then leased to franchises. This successful program may be expanded from 10% of the Fund's portfolio to 33% and is based on the Entrepreneurial objective of obtaining a return on investment of at least the inflation rate plus 5%. In a different area, upon noting the failure of the stock market to keep up with the inflation rate of the 1970s, the largest American stockbroker, Merrill Lynch and Company, adopted an Entrepreneurial acquisitions strategy to diversify its business, purchasing everything from real estate to insurance in order to further the new corporate objective: to provide a shopping mall of financial services and to obtain a percentage of virtually every financial transaction a client makes.[46]

Other institutional investors, seeking ways to tie their funds to hard assets to protect them from inflation, have turned to Mexican bonds indexed to the price of oil and French bonds hooked to the price of gold, both introduced by the government.[47]

The purchase of foreign bonds is just one tactic in another major Entrepreneurial strategy: foreign expansion. Frank Hoenemeyr, executive vice president of Prudential Insurance Company, projects that foreign bonds might be in the position now that real estate was ten years ago as far as American insurance company portfolio and pension fund managers are concerned. American law sets penalties for pension fund managers who invest imprudently. But new interpretations of the U.S. Employee Retirement Income Security Act and the 1970s rise in the inflation rate have caused Maintenance managers to become more Entrepreneurial: They now worry that they might be considered imprudent if they do not diversify their portfolios into other currencies.[48]

Of course corporations have two ultimate foreign expansion strategies: direct foreign investment and going multinational. Evidence indicates that domestic rather than foreign factors constitute the primary motivating influences for direct foreign investment.[49] And within a given industry, the multinationals are almost always the leading domestic producers.[50] Oligopolies seek continued growth in both absolute size and share of the market and desire to gain access to raw materials and cheap labor. Foreign investment proposals are usually considered or initiated by lower management echelons (where the Entrepreneurial impetus seems to have shifted today) who tend to overstate the benefits and understate the costs of investments they recommend until the top levels of Maintenance managers clip the suggestions down to size.[51] Despite such Maintenance hesitation, multinational corporations control between a quarter and a third of all world production. About one-fourth of world foreign investment is in developing countries, and 70% of this investment is in only fifteen countries--basically those with convenient, stable economic environments offering tax incentives, large markets, cheap labor and easy access to oil or other natural resources.[52] Internationally the poorest developing countries hardest hit by the inflationary impact of oil and other price rises are forced into Defeatist and Free Rider strategies by default, much as the poor and unemployed are domestically. Corporations and established institutions (and individuals who are relatively well-off) are best positioned to be able to afford the prerequisites for effective Maintenance and Entrepreneurial strategies although some small firms have succeeded under conditions of stagflation due to their greater flexibility. One reason is that the corporate strategies that appear to function most smoothly are based on well-to-do and stable states, such as Japan and West Germany, where Maintenance functions in terms of restraining inflation can often be taken for granted through effective state responsibility, freeing private (and "public-private") corporations from some of their own Maintenance costs so that they can focus more intensely upon Entrepreneurship and changing export markets.

Take the heuristic case of Toyo Kogya, the Mazda automaking company based in Hiroshima, which illustrates how much of Japanese industry was able to cope with the economic difficulties of the 1970s with growth, little inflation and virtually no unemployment, creating a basis for Entrepreneurial expansion in the 1980s. Toyo Kogya faced the threat of going under five years ago as Chrysler and British Leyland do at present: It was an overstaffed, mismanaged producer of gas-guzzling cars. By the 1980s the company restructured to more than double its productivity and to cut its debt in half without firing a worker. The traditional loyalty of the Japanese local community, labor force and private creditors which made this reversal possible was due in no small part to the typical Japanese Maintenance principle of guaranteeing that no one will lose their job, giving management in crisis a much freer hand in radical reorganization and technological innovation with cooperative team-work participation on the part of labor. Management compromised significantly in letting the Sumitomo Bank appoint six of its people to major positions, including chairman. This assured the financial basis for the restructuring strategy--cutting back parts inventories despite the risk of stopping the assembly line, investing in new equipment to improve efficiency in the weak spots (including robots), freezing new hiring, agreeing to accept smaller wage rises, rerouting several thousand unneeded workers on the assembly lines to serve temporarily as Mazda car salesmen at distribution centers and from door-to-door. Many of the suggestions came from the workers themselves, through a system of "worker participation groups," each made up of eight to ten employees who meet regularly to suggest new efficiency and productivity measures. Japan's great world lead in the use and development of robots is just one indicator that the Toyo Kogya case is not unique: Maintenance-Entrepreneurial blends such as the simultaneous introduction of robots with the guarantee that no one will lose a job make Japan perhaps the optimum Western corporate society in terms of inflation-fighting and technological advancement with minimum social cost. Companies in other countries may want to consider adapting to some of the Japanese innovations. Whereas in earlier periods inflation was accepted as prerequisite to innovation, with a few notable exceptions such as Toyo Kogya, modern inflationary phases appear to stimulate conservative Maintenance strategies in order to reduce uncertainty to the point of excluding the creative, risk-taking Entrepreneurial strategies necessary for coping effectively in the long-run with the rapid change we are experiencing.

VIII.

STATE ANTI-INFLATION POLICIES

VIII. STATE ANTI-INFLATION POLICIES

> "An inevitable consequence of an inflationary economy is an increasing concentration of political power, as more and more people are willing to accept less and less personal freedom in exchange for a little more order in their lives."
>
> --F. Harvey Popell

The more one moves from an individual to a collective level of analysis, the greater the diffusion of interests, and the less the likelihood that anyone will be satisfied. As one proceeds from individual portfolios to corporate strategies and from there to government policies, clear-cut private interests become increasingly obscure leaving an enigma behind called "the public good." And often the resulting government policies, which should be encouraging entrepreneurship as a means of reversing declining productivity and economic growth rates, serve rather to add to the uncertainty, turning citizens into Defeatists and Free Riders and businesspeople into conservative Maintenance Men. Through Jacobinist promises to satisfy everyone's needs in the past, the Western democratic nation-state has increased the mystique of inflation and undermined its own legitimacy in the present.[53] Indeed, some of the most successful Entrepreneurial strategies of individuals and private institutions have been based on the assumption that the government would never be able to keep its promises to control inflation and, therefore, one should either invest in inflation through hard assets or spread one's risks internationally in order to be able to play the effects of the few competent state anti-inflation policies against the much more numerous incompetent ones. One way many people did this in the decade of the 1970s was to buy German marks and Swiss francs, indirectly pushing the very reluctant Germans and Swiss in the direction of sponsoring international reserve currencies, partially displacing the discredited American dollar.

West Germany and Switzerland have been exceptionally effective in fighting inflation, and, therefore, may serve as a useful point of departure in examining the elements of successful state anti-inflation policies. Both of these nations managed to hold consumer price increases down to an average of little more than 5% in the 1970s, compared to about 7% for the United States and 8½% for all the OECD countries (from 1970-1978). In both cases, this success appears to be due more to the domestic environment in which policy was made than to inherently superior techniques of monetary control or fiscal dexterity. The Swiss and German central banks are not, in short, models to be easily copied by others. For example, a Bank of England study of seven Western nations which began setting monetary targets between 1974 and 1976 concluded:

> Judged solely by whether the targets were met, the results have been generally poor. Only Canada has consistently met its targets. The United Kingdom has had one failure in three; the United States has overshot between one-third and one-half of the targets set, depending upon which aggregate is considered; Switzerland and Italy have overshot more often than not; while Germany and France have not yet met a target. There has been no obvious difference between the performance of countries with narrow and broad aggregate targets.[54]

But if almost everyone failed to meet their national monetary targets, including the Germans and Swiss, at least half the time, what distinguishes the successful from the unsuccessful central bank strategy? The answer, very simply, is that the targets so often missed by the central banks of Germany and Switzerland were <u>much lower</u> than those missed by the other central banks. During the late 1970s target ranges for the mix of aggregates selected by the seven central banks extended from 5-6% in Switzerland and about 8% in Germany, to 12% in the United States, the United Kingdom and France, 15% in Canada, and up to 46% in Italy.[55] The crucial question then becomes: What factors allowed the Germans and Swiss to set monetary targets so much lower than the rest?

Perhaps the most important prerequisite for a successful anti-inflation policy which Switzerland and West Germany illustrate <u>par excellence</u> is domestic stability. Self-serving democratic politicians often promise that their anti-inflation policies will <u>bring</u> domestic stability, whereas it may be just the other way around: that effective anti-inflation policies flow <u>from</u> domestic stability. West Germany and

Switzerland have a number of features in common (too often taken for granted or ignored by economists) that facilitate domestic stability: (1) They are two of the richest countries in the world (in terms of per capita income, among the 24 leading industrial countries of the non-Communist world in 1979, Switzerland ranked first with $13,450, and West Germany fourth with $10,420--in contrast, for example, with the United States which ranked ninth with $9,660);[56] (2) Both societies have conservative, Maintenance political cultures, seeking to coopt change into the existing equilibrium to preserve stability;[57] (3) They both have effective democratic social contracts that reduce the potential for political polarization within their societies (despite its apparent imminence) often to the point of making them appear to be "apolitical" in the 1970s compared to others (like Italy or the United States);* (4) There is a widespread anti-inflation consensus among both populations; (5) Certain aspects of their domestic markets are "closed" (restricted to insiders), making them more easily manageable in terms of disruptive foreign influences and serving as a basis of effective foreign exchange rate policies; (6) Until recently, both countries have been able to import foreign labor when needed, and to turn off the flow when it became economically inconvenient;[58] (7) Relatively speaking, both are homogeneous, small- to medium-sized countries and are more manageable and less vulnerable in certain ways than large, heterogeneous nations (and particularly than the United States with its responsibilities as a superpower and as a defender of a world reserve currency).

Apart from these critical, broad similarities, there are, of course, significant differences between the German and Swiss experiences, for example in their techniques of monetary control. These differences highlight the variations of the relationship between a

---

*Although the West German society may be approaching a stalemate, there is still a widespread conservative consensus as demonstrated by the Christian Democratic landslide in the 1983 national elections. See R. Isaak, "The German Industrial Model Under Siege," in _Adherent_, Volume 10, No. 3, Spring, 1983. Also see Peter J. Katzenstein, "Capitalism in One Country?: Switzerland in the International Economy," in _International Organization_, Vol. 34, No. 4, Fall, 1980.

particular society's democratic political culture and its financial policy. In late 1974 the German government attempted to persuade the trade unions to agree to wage restraints in return for the assurance of price stability. To make this policy credible the government asked the Deutsche Bundesbank to start setting monetary targets. The central bank reluctantly agreed and until mid-1977 stayed reasonably close to its targets. But skepticism arose among Maintenance Men in 1978 as a result of a significant overshooting of the basic target for "central bank money," made up of circulating currency and the bank's minimum reserves minus cash held by banks. According to Mendelsohn, this overshooting was the result of the Bundesbank's inability to reconcile its exchange rate and monetary growth objectives.[59] In 1979, the bank came again much closer to its target.

The Bundesbank functions by focusing on the reserve base of the banking system, imposing minimum reserves at different levels on the liability of banks according to their type, location, size, kind of liability and the maturity of the liability. For example, German banks have been required to maintain reserves of up to 100 per cent against Deutschmark liabilities to non-residents, effectively halting this kind of flow into the Deutschmark. One reason for the emphasis on the reserve base of the German central bank is that German authorities have only a limited scope for open market policy. As Professor Stanley Black notes:

> The Bundesbank ... has a substantial degree of independence, but it has a closer partnership with the federal government and the Ministry of Finance than is the case in the United States. There is need for closer coordination in Germany, because the relatively narrower government securities market means that the bulk of government surpluses and deficits are reflected in changes in bank loans to the government, with direct effects on the money supply itself. Furthermore, the limited possibilities for open market operations have meant that changes in reserve requirements and the availability of central bank lending have been the primary tools to influence banks' behavior. The external constraint has played a much larger role in Germany, where settlement of very large balance-

of-payments surpluses prior to 1973 has been in the form of changes in foreign reserves which add directly to the liquidity of the banking system. Thus, while independent and free to follow goals of macroeconomic balance, in practice the Bundesbank has had a much more constricted range of instruments and field of action.[60]

Switzerland's central bank is even more limited than Germany's in its scope for open market operations since there is almost no domestic money market. Taxes in the Swiss Confederation are subject to approval by referendum, almost precluding an active Swiss fiscal policy and therefore putting the brunt of national anti-inflation policy on the central bank. But even the monetary authorities find their options limited by democracy in Switzerland, given the high political sensitivity to home mortgage rates and the rates at which cantons borrow from the domestic market. The dollar is the normal medium of exchange between Swiss banks and if it is necessary to reduce liquidity resulting from open market activities, the central bank issues paper "sterilization prescriptions" for this purpose. Given the country's great domestic stability and manageability (due to the anti-inflation consensus, etc.), Swiss monetary policy is mainly concerned with neutralizing foreign inflows through a wide range of controls (for example, purchase of Swiss property by non-residents is possible only after five years of residence and permission for residence is difficult to obtain). Apart from the investment in the Swiss franc debt of other non-residents, foreigners find no other Swiss franc investments available and are usually required to convert any proceeds from borrowing out of the Swiss franc on receipt. The dollar crisis of 1978 upset the system and its targets momentarily, but only (as in the German case) when an uncomfortable compromise had to be reached between monetary growth and exchange rate objectives.[61]

West Germany, Switzerland and Austria (a derivation of the German strategy) represent islands of stability in an inflation-riddled world of change. Using domestic consensus and social need satisfaction as a stable base, conservative West German and Swiss Maintenance Men then turn to the international market for auxiliary "Free Rider" and "Entrepreneurial" strategies. As Free Riders they often have dumped unwanted costs on others--by exporting foreign labor that is no longer needed, for example. As Entrepreneurs they have used a relatively stable, "apolitical" base as a platform for export-oriented growth. Foreign trade, for example, accounts for more than one-third of West Germany's gross national product and one West German worker in five owes his or her job to exports.[62] Figure VIII-1 illustrates several "ideal types" of state strategies in inflationary periods, all of which West Germany and Switzerland have utilized in a subtle, Maintenance-grounded strategy mix.

Drawing on their less than liberal domestic bases, the Swiss and Germans have developed an orderly role for their Entrepreneurs and workers that furthers economic growth without overstimulating inflation. Perhaps the most notorious example of this is the West German management-labor codetermination policy, or Mitbestimmung. According to the 1976 legislation, workers and employers in major industrial firms of over 2,000 people have roughly equal parity on a policy supervisory board (management having one extra vote in case of a tie). The 1980 conflict between Mannesmann-Konzerns and the union IG Metall evolved because the company wanted to reorganize in such a way as to fall below the 2,000 limit to improve productivity and get around the codetermination category it was in. But significantly this conflict thus far has been handled through negotiation rather than through violence or long strikes--evidence of relative West German "union docility" in comparison with other countries (such as Italy) where such codetermination laws for cooperative industrial democracy do not yet exist.[63] A Maintenance strategy thus coopts both managers and workers for the sake of domestic stability, who then make long-term Entrepreneurial plans together for the sake of the company and economic growth. Japan's systems of worker participation have similar effects. A low rate of inflation and a steady rate of economic growth may well be correlates of a successful codetermination policy.

In other less Maintenance-oriented political structures, such as the United States, steady central bank policies and the creation of codetermination legislation do not appear to be feasible political objectives. One can even hypothesize that the more explicitly Entrepreneurial a political culture is supposed to be in an ideological sense, the more

Figure VIII-1

IDEAL TYPES OF STATE STRATEGIES IN INFLATIONARY PERIODS	Time Perspective	Risk Orientation	Concrete Strategies or Policies
FREE RIDER	Present-oriented	High risks at low cost	-Focus on exporting domestic costs to others, on loans, on postponing payments, on exploiting the international arena for short-term benefits, i.e. devaluations -Indexation; agricultural subsidies -Government subsidies for lame-duck industries -Periodically tapping IMF, others, for loans -Wage and Price controls when necessary -Selected protectionism when advantageous
MAINTENANCE	Present-Middle-range Future	Limited risks at moderate cost	-Focus on coopting change to keep costs and benefits in balance for stability -Use of voluntary wage and price guidelines -Tight monetary and fiscal policies as needed -Preservation of steady exchange rate -Stress on balanced federal budget -Simultaneous cuts in taxes and government spending -Elimination of excessive imported labor, immigration limits -Codetermination policy with unions and management
ENTREPRENEURIAL	Future-oriented	High risks even at high cost	-Focus on outwitting the future with extraordinary achievement, productivity, innovation -Elimination of indexation -Eliminationof subsidies for lame-duck industries, farms, agriculture -Pay-offs to stimulate productivity and export-oriented growth (through tax cuts, etc.) -Eliminate double-tax on corporate gains, encourage long-term capital investment, R & D -Support accelerated depreciation based on replacement cost -State subsidies for long-range technological breakthroughs -Anti-trust legislation and seek money for starting small businesses

difficult it is to create the stable domestic consensus necessary to foster effective Entrepreneurship in the international market. The residue of laissez-faire liberalism in the American culture appears to make the United States particularly vulnerable to shifts in the business and electoral cycles, which more Maintenance-oriented societies such as the German, Swiss and Japanese can better "manage." The trade-off for stimulating individual incentive and Entrepreneurship seems to be narrow self-interest in terms of group bargaining at the national level that satisfies neither the groups in question nor the national interest.

Take the case of the American central bank. When the Federal Reserve shifted radically from monetary control through interest rates to control through the banking system's reserve base and severely tightened the money supply in October of 1979, the foreign financial reaction was positive, believing this would stabilize the high American inflation rate and strengthen the dollar. But domestically, many American politicians (and businesspeople for that matter), interpreted this move to halt inflation by deliberately creating a recession to be a desperate step by President Jimmy Carter after his voluntary wage and price guideline policy failed. By April 1980 interest rates soared to a prime rate of 20% and a rate on 90-day certificates of deposit that topped 18%, jolting nearly everyone.

The auto and housing industries tail-spinned into a near depression, pulling the United States into a recession that ran both too late and too deep for President Carter's political health in an election year. His economic advisors had greatly underestimated the American consumer's intention to keep on spending, stimulating the economy and slowing down the arrival of the recession. The average American saving rate dropped to about 3% as Americans spent their money before it lost even more value against a double-digit inflation rate, clearly not having any confidence in the government at all in terms of controlling inflation. Then Paul Volcker, Chairman of the Federal Reserve Board, loosened the money supply, letting the prime interest rate fall to 11% by mid-summer of 1980, hoping to reverse the recession quickly, no doubt in order to help Carter's re-election chances as well. As Senior Economist for Bankers Trust in New York noted:

> What we have seen so far is a flip-flop policy--first too tight, then too loose. The Fed is now stimulating the money supply in order to counteract its earlier tightening, and just at a time when everyone in Washington is talking about a tax cut. In short, we could wind up ... with a new surge in inflation and a stagnant economy--a British-style stagflation that would be the worst of both worlds.[64]

"Interest rate roulette" is not unusual in the American experience and does not bode well for a stable anti-inflation policy in the future. Karen W. Arenson summed this up: "For decades, the American economy has ridden up and down on business cycles. With each cycle, interest rates have soared, peaking at levels above those of the previous cycle. And when they have descended, it was not quite to the previous lows."[65] Democratic pressures no doubt help push up the base level of interest rates as well as the inflation rates over time, a sort of awkward collusion between business cycle and electoral cycle management that as often as not represents the maximization of the private interests of politicians and business and labor leaders at the long-term cost of the public interest.[66] All too often the liberal American democratic culture yields a schizophrenic strategy mix in inflation policy ranging from extreme Enterpreneurial incentives to outright Free Rider hand-outs. For the Americans "Maintenance" appears to be an uncomfortable, frustrating half-way house between what are perceived to be basic socio-economic rights and the promise of upward mobility, between a humane, democratic concern for those at the bottom of the ladder and a meritocratic commitment to give occasional incentives to exceptionally creative and productive individuals who can produce the economic growth necessary to pay for the redistribution already promised and who can keep the social escalator going.

Most, if not all, of the solutions to the American inflation dilemma proposed for the future fail to take the limits of the American political culture sufficiently into account. The economists advocating voluntary wage and price guidelines "enforced" by a larger Council on Wage and Price Stability find themselves frustrated by higher political decisions made by the Pay Advisory Committee that loosens the guidelines to accommodate representatives of big unions and big business (thus on January 22, 1980 this committee replaced the original 7% standard with a range of 7.5% to 9.5%--a new standard higher than many collective bargainers had even aimed for in wage hikes).[67] The balanced federal budget advocated by Presidents Carter and Reagan and economist Alan Greenspan, among others, is a utopian dream in a period of recession, high unemployment, inflation, public pressures for tax cuts and increased federal spending for defense. Equally unfeasible politically is the call for a tax-based incomes policy (TIP) by Federal Reserve Board Governor Henry Wallich and economist Sidney Weintraub, and the late Arthur Okun: It is inconceivable to believe that union and business lobbyists in Congress would not adamantly and effectively oppose any legislative attempt to use the tax system to hold pay increases to 5% per annum when the future rate of inflation is apt to exceed that rate.[68] The John K. Galbraith-Edward Kennedy advocacy of wage and price controls not only lacks political support, but is a Free Rider strategy in disguise--thump wages and prices down with a big stick in the short-term to get everyone's attention, postponing the high bill for such controls to a later date when the controls bureaucracy would have to be paid for and when inflation would skyrocket as controls were lifted. Even more blatantly in the Free Rider category is economist Milton Friedman's surprising support for indexation (presumably balanced by his Maintenance call for simultaneous cuts in taxes and government spending).[69]

The Free Rider nature of indexation is perhaps best illustrated by the cases of Israel and Iceland where almost everything is indexed to the rise in the cost of living from wages and prices to subsidies and interest rates. At well over 100% inflation, the Israelis must run in place faster, but they have the comfort of knowing that the national debt and their own spending is made up of paper spent now that will be even less valuable in the future--meaning a relative gain, as debts will be cheaper in real value when they need to be paid back. Of course such indexation and inflation cause widespread rigidities in the economic system, frustrating the Entrepreneurial strategy to the point that many young entrepreneurs leave Israel to seek more flexible opportunities abroad, even if they plan to return later in their lives. Furthermore, established business people and the government appear to have disproportionate advantages in the art of profiting from an inflation rate that reached 135 percent in 1980, whereas the average Israeli citizen struggles just to keep up, losing almost one-tenth in the value of individual take-home pay despite cost-of-living payments to counterbalance inflation (according to the Central Bureau of Statistics for 1980). The businessman can profit from inflation by delaying payments on checks he writes for a month or two, and companies with hundreds of employees can make a killing by delaying all payments to the government for taxes and social security withholding. In a half-hearted effort to deter such practices, the Israeli Finance Ministry quadrupled the penalty from ¼ of one percent to one percent weekly on overdue taxes in 1981. Yet, the government, too, benefits by paying its debts late, largely because citizens are delinquent in paying theirs. In sum, the fine art of profiting from inflation in Israel is apt to continue in ways implicitly condoned by the state, making widespread Israeli indexation a stimulant to a kind of collective "Free Rider strategy" based on the principle that the more you owe the richer you get.

In Iceland, since everything is indexed, no individual (at least in theory) is disproportionately disadvantaged by the recent 60% inflation rate. Iceland manages to keep this sytem going by devaluing the national currency whenever it is necessary to keep its exports competitive and by long-term foreign borrowing (which the nation can continue for a long time given its good credit rating, if it can maintain its low debt service ratio). However, the country was jolted by the oil price hikes of the 1970s, which contributed to a quadrupling of its inflation rate. To become less oil-dependent upon the Soviet Union, Icelandic state managers are negotiating long-term, fixed-price contracts with the British North Seas Oil Corporation. And as a psychological, anti-inflation Maintenance tactic, in 1981 the government dropped two zeros off the kronur's value--from about 440 kronur to a dollar to 4.4.[70] But undoubtedly the only reason that Israel and Iceland can get away with their heavy dependence on the Free Rider strategy is that they are small states of strategic importance with good credit-worthiness in a rapidly changing international system.

IX.

DEMOCRATIC PARADOXES IN A CHANGING INTERNATIONAL SYSTEM

IX. DEMOCRATIC PARADOXES IN A CHANGING INTERNATIONAL SYSTEM

"*Demere rebus tumultus*"

--Seneca

From the individual to the corporation to the state--the ultimate abstraction and reification in this inevitable process of diffusion comes in going finally from the level of the state to that of the international system.[71] At the global level few individual interests can be satisfied, corporations enter the high-risk realm of multinational gambling, and most national interests are fated to be frustrated with little relief. From the international perspective, as poet Wallace Stevens put it, "the world is ugly and the people are sad."

Inflation is a rich man's preoccupation: The poor have few, if any, valuable resources to protect against the loss of value and have little choice or control of strategies to defend what they do have. With the exception of the oil-producers, developing nations are usually forced into a Defeatist-Free Rider strategy: Mere Maintenance, not wealth-creating Entrepreneurship, is their daily dream. Even the rich industrial democracies of the West found the 1970s hard to cope with and as often as not became mired in Maintenance, paddling upstream in the flood of change with obsolete equipment. The greater the perceived or anticipated social change, the more the conservative impulse to preserve the status quo pushed policy options in Western democracies up to the superstructural level of stalemated government, union and corporate bargaining and the more difficult collective learning or adaptation became.[72]

Economic theories of rational expectations normally underestimate the human resistance to change, which may well make short-term sense for a number of individuals and interest groups. For example, President Carter's assumption in 1979 that American consumers would stop spending as interest rates rose proved to be premature, and Prime Minister Margaret Thatcher's operating principle that unions can be persuaded to accept drops in the real wages of their workers for the sake of the Queen's own country has proved to be problematic.[73] Sometimes the lack of meaningful dialogue among groups in Western democracies reminds one of the three monkeys: The government sees no evil (and continues to pretend), the unions hear no evil (and press wage demands regardless of what others tell them about the condition of the economy), and the consumers speak no evil (not bothering to protest about government policies they oppose out of cynicism or because they have found unofficial loopholes that allow them to continue to do as they like).

The ability of a nation to adapt effectively to the barrage of exogenous shocks of the 1970s--the breakdown of the Bretton Woods system, the initiation of flexible exchange rates, the skyrocketing prices of oil and other commodities, among others--depended upon the patterns of popular resistance to change manifest in the indigenous political culture as well as upon the bargaining power of the state in the world economy. For example, cross-country econometric studies suggest that a hypothetical 25% increase in the unemployment rate results in a great percentage of reduction in the rate of change of wages in Canada, France and Japan, and to a lesser but still significant extent in West Germany. In contrast, wages appear to be much less sensitive to the unemployment rate in Great Britain, and even less so in Italy and the United States. This data implies that workers in Italy, the United Kingdom and the United States base their resistance to a reduction in the real wage on the concept of a "fair wage" derived from both their own past wage and the wages of others. Since people do not easily change the concepts on which they base their behavior, it follows under this hypothesis that attempts to reduce inflation by increasing unemployment are bound to be slow and painful.[74]

On the other hand, the evidence suggests that in Canada, France, Japan and West Germany,

> resistance to reducing real wages will continue only as long as the authorities continue to expand the money supply and achieve additional output to absorb the unemployed. A restrictive monetary policy--announced by the government--will lead workers to accept short-run reductions in their real wage because behavior will change when a decrease in aggregate demand is anticipated and workers realize they are overestimating the domestic rate of inflation. This

> theory implies, therefore, that expectations about the inflation rate can be altered relatively quickly and at little unemployment cost by a government which decides to implement a restrictive monetary policy.[75]

Productivity growth rates, the power of trade unions, and the traditions of political economic culture are among the factors that affect this wage-employment relationship. "For instance, there is concern in Italy and the United Kingdom when unemployment rises; but in Japan or the Federal Republic of Germany there is concern when the inflation rate rises," notes IMF economist Marion Bond.[76]

Due to underlying structural continuities, high growth rates during the 1950s and 1960s generally enabled Western democratic governments to be successful in making up any lack of demand that did temporarily occur in their economies to the extent that these economies remained relatively flexible. Income and living standards rose rapidly with successful demand management and policy-makers were concerned with equity and income distribution without worrying much about evolving economic inefficiencies. But the exogenous shocks of the 1970s and the resulting flood of liquidity and drop in economic growth rates shifted policy priorities from equity to efficiency concerns in the West. However, for a number of countries--Great Britain and the United States, for example--the shift came too late in terms of maintaining a flexible and stable domestic economy capable of competing with nations that had more consistently balanced equity and efficiency concerns--West Germany and Japan, for instance. Domestic rigidities preventing flexible adjustment to the new international environment abounded. High minimum wage thresholds had to be paid for by a less than vibrant national product. OECD countries were pushed towards productivity as machines replaced low-level-function jobs and a whole category of least-skilled people were put out of work.

Unions developed a "leveling policy" at the upper end of the wage scale leaving too narrow a gap between the highest and lowest paid workers, eliminating incentives for training for more skilled jobs. Thus, the unions inadvertently reinforced the <u>structure</u> of unemployment in OECD nations which shows high unemployment in trained areas. Restriction from dismissal from firms caught in economic decline made for further rigidities. Traditionally, such job security was affected not domestically, but internationally by protecting products and jobs at the borders. But the GATT free trade rounds and pledges prevented such protectionism in the 1970s in most cases, and OECD governments found themselves under pressure to do things domestically that would have the same effect as tariffs at the borders.[77] Certain weak private industries received subsidies, not to mention nationalized industries. Taxes were the sources of these subsidies, taken not from corporate losses but from the profitable corporations, from the dynamic side of the economy. International uncertainties and government tax burdens and regulations trapped many companies in mere Maintenance strategies for the sake of their survival, often leaving little capital or incentive over for long-term capital investment and research and development. Until a belated change in policy priorities on the part of a few in the late 1970s, OECD governments were often supporting the stagnant parts of their economies rather than trying to eliminate them. Democracy reinforces this tendency towards non-adjustment since politically it is easier to focus on concrete job losses than it is to stress the more nebulous gains due to productivity increases or subsidies for long-term research and development.[78]

The nations that did the best in the 1970s era of flexible exchange rates were the hard-currency countries capable of protecting themselves against imported inflation (or of exporting inflation to others) by revaluing their currencies, using export controls or reducing import barriers. Weak currency countries, on the other hand, found themselves more often concerned with exporting unemployment than with inflation fighting, which they attempted to do by devaluing their currencies, imposing import controls and establishing export subsidies. Both strong and weak currency states were motivated by self-protection (or Maintenance fears) in the turbulence of the 1970s--the former, by protection from inflation, the latter, by protection from unemployment. Both tended to see through the money illusions of an inflationary period, but to adjust their "real expectations" in terms of different predominant conservative impulses.

For example, West Germany, a leading hard-currency country, became a skillful player of "the floating game," appreciating the Deutschmark vis-à-vis the competing foreign currencies, but not to the level of global inflation, thus protecting itself from imported inflation while preserving the competitive price of its exports. As Wilhelm Hankel and the economists of the Kiel Institut für Weltwirtschaft have demonstrated, this West German revaluation strategy assured the nation of its foreign trade position by means of a relative sacrifice in its real terms of trade.[79] Or, one could say that West Germany's effective Maintenance strategy depends upon hooking its currency as a Free Rider upon the world inflation rate, but then bringing it down a few notches out of a healthy respect for Entrepreneurship (reflected in its export dynamism).

Austria's strategy, to take another example, was a variation on the Deutschmark theme. Rather than taking the temptation of other deficit countries of depreciating its currency (downward floating) and thereby importing inflation rather than stability and forfeiting the real foundation of its foreign credits, Austria maintained a hard schilling policy, using the inflated international capital market to continue financing its badly needed domestic restructuring and development and blessing Austria with a state of full employment without inflation. Due to its capital imports and reserve growth, Austria imported stability rather than inflation and therefore could not export inflation. As Hankel has noted:

> Since receipts and purchases--thanks to the rise in the schilling vis-à-vis the U.S. dollar--were calculated at domestic rates, which were far below the U.S. dollar-denominated world market prices, this portion of international credit creation did not intensify either objectively demonstrable or subjectively expected price thrusts. On the contrary, the foreign financiers acquired their schilling claims because they saw future stable profits rather than inflationary losses--neither domestic losses due to higher prices nor external losses due to currency depreciation (which, given its debt, would also be far too expensive for Austria). As a result, Austria's foreign debt offers the rare example of a stability-conforming loan.[80]

Austria thus might be viewed as a Responsible Free Rider--one with stabilizing Maintenance effects both at home and abroad.

Another illustrative example of the reaction of strong and weak currency nations to the uncertainties of the floating system of exchange rates initiated in 1971 and the inflation of the 1970s connected with the decline of the dollar was the agreement to create the European Monetary System (EMS) in 1978. Stimulated initially by Roy Jenkins, President of the European Commission, West German Chancellor Helmut Schmidt and French President Giscard d'Estaing presented the rest of the European Community with a fait accomplis, extending the former European "snake in the tunnel" system of keeping regional currencies within a 2.25 range of fluctuation from each other to a "parity grid system." The German motivation was largely defensive--to protect the Deutschmark from revaluing to too high a level, as was threatened by the dollar crisis of 1977, in order to spread out the responsibility for currency stabilization among all the Common Market nations--expanding "the DMZ" (the Deutschmark zone). The French, who have always longed nostalgically for a return to a system of fixed exchange rates, hoped a parity grid EMS would create an external pressure for monetary discipline within Europe and buffer Europe's independence somewhat from the flip-flops of American economic policy. The weak currency countries, such as Italy and Great Britain, demanded a "basket system" made up of the weighted average of all currencies in the system, which would be more flexible given their domestic economic difficulties. A Belgian compromise combined the systems successfully, although the British did not join it for domestic political and economic reasons (except for linking the pound to the basket as an indicator of divergence) and the Italians were granted a 6% instead of a 2.25% range of flexibility within the parity grid.[81] The European unit of account or Ecu used by central banks within the EMS has worked well enough to be extended in the 1980s as an international monetary mechanism, perhaps eventually becoming the basis for a European currency.[82]

However, the starting parity values of the European Monetary System were based upon the dollar's value, and one could argue that the EMS worked in the late 1970s and early 1980s only to the extent that the dollar has stabilized. That is, the independence of the EMS may be illusory and more deeply linked to American domestic economic policy than the Europeans would like to admit. Additionally, the meaningfulness of the EMS is thrown into doubt by the wide divergence of domestic inflation rates within the system, on the one hand (witness the March, 1983 EMS crisis precipitated by France) and by the system's dependence upon external OPEC and xeno market fluctuations, on the other hand. The European "joint float" is useful in reducing the level of uncertainty in an often unpredictable international monetary environment, but its stabilizing value is extremely relative and may have the unhealthy side-effect of giving domestic European economies an excuse not to make badly needed structural changes to cope with the future trends of the world economy.[83] In this sense, the EMS itself may prove to be a sort of "money illusion."

The analysis of individual, corporate and state levels of anti-inflation strategies above implies a number of things about future prospects for Western industrial democracies. First, the built-in, "sub-rational" reactions of different democratic cultures that determine the domestic patterns of resistance to flexible adjustment will most likely continue to predominate in the future (and will continue to be underestimated in importance by pure economists). States that are apt to be most successful in coping with inflation are those that are (1) wealthy, (2) of limited geographical size, (3) with a stable "apolitical" domestic base that coopts potential management-labor conflicts, (4) with a wide-spread anti-inflation consensus in the population, (5) capable of limiting their vulnerability to exogeneous shocks and imported inflation without simultaneously undermining the incentives for productivity and entrepreneurship. These West Germanys, Switzerlands, Japans and Austrias, however, are not only less than "pure democracies" (in the polarized, political outspoken sense of everyone participating all the time in decisions) but are exceptions to the rule for the nation-state system as a whole and for the OECD countries in particular. As "models" they suggest that even among rich industrial democracies there may be a "take-off" point which makes effective anti-inflation policies possible, which depends upon extra-democratic factors some of which appear to be unchangeable (i.e. geography).

Second, above this sub-rational level of probable national reactions, the liberal democratic ideology of the West that promises the individual the freedom to maximize his or her own interests appears to be stimulated by inflation while simultaneously undermining the socio-economic conditions that make individual social mobility possible. The maximum pay-offs for the individual in the 1970s went to those who invested in hard assets--in real estate, stamps or gold--not to those who invested in the stock market--providing long-term capital investment badly needed for productivity and research and development in society. Inflation seemed to improve the life-chances of very few people, but had the effect of speeding up the tempo of every-day life and making everyone more aware of material and social scarcity without significantly changing the social distances among classes--like an escalator turned on high speed. The increasing tempo and uncertainty of life in the 1970s left the unemployed, the old and the poor torn between Defeatist and Free Rider strategies, while even those who could afford to aim for the optimum Maintenance-Entrepreneurial strategy mix were unnerved by the flood of change and often regressed to senile Maintenance-security preoccupations, mixed with Free Rider and Defeatist tendencies. As chairman of the Expansion Publishing Group, F. Harvey Popell noted:

> The real tragedy of inflation is that it creates an economic framework that makes it practically impossible to achieve a unity of interests between the individual and society as a whole .... When an economic system does not work, as is the case when inflation continues unabated, moral values develop that justify the individual's struggle for survival in an increasingly hostile environment, values that tend to aggravate the very conditions against which the individual is trying to protect himself.[84]

Corporations, too, were overwhelmed with the economic dislocations of the 1970s and often became bogged down in self-defeating Maintenance thinking that did not sufficiently prepare or invest for the future--as in the case of the American automobile manufacturers, whose failure to keep up with the foreign competition helped to bring on the American recession of 1980, slowing down other economies in the Western world and putting aid to lesser developed countries on the back burner. As individuals and companies continue to fail in the competitive environment of the 1980s, the question is whether or not the democratic state is apt to pick up the bill of the losers without giving them training for future self-sufficiency, perhaps turning even the majority into "Free Riders" of one sort of another: the poor, the old, the unemployed, the sick, the large lame-duck industries, the public services and institutions in deficit. Such state policies, in turn, can create a fiscal drag and rigidities that make it increasingly difficult for the state to adjust to changes in the international environment.

Nor has the ostensible "independence" of central banks in states like West Germany and the United States proved to be an adequate means to achieve "inflation-free growth" (which may well be a contradiction in terms). The open market operations of the Bundesbank were limited to begin with and the European Monetary System has served to further curtail the central bank's autonomy and control of the West German economy. The U.S. Federal Reserve is riding upon a whirlwind of democratic pressures and interest group conflicts, making it difficult for the bank to control either interest rates or money aggregates with a consistent policy for a long enough period of time to be effective. Raising interest rates to counter inflation by reducing the money in circulation seems to have a dampening effect upon investment, and therefore upon Entrepreneurship and productivity--the long-term cures for inflation and unemployment. On the other hand, reducing interest rates to stimulate investment fans inflation in the short-run. The 1979 policy shift of Paul Volcker, Chairman of the Federal Reserve, away from a stress in interest rates and to a focus on money aggregates or reserves was initially promising but proved to be illusory as fiscal pressures undermined Volcker's control and helped to stimulate flip-flops in this policy. A constitutional amendment to counter such pressures by banning government budget deficits is probably unviable politically in an age of American military build-up and even if passed would just stimulate more off-budget credit financing, including loans and loan guarantees which have already climbed to over 550 billion dollars.[85] And even under the best political circumstances, central bank economists may not know enough in the changing environment to make accurate predictions and sound long-term policies. For example, the popular reliance of monetarists in the United States upon M1-B (currency plus all deposits subject to check withdrawals) as the basic indicator in charting monetary targets in the early 1980s is very slippery since it does not include checks drawn on money-market funds for large-ticket purchases--a behavior that is apt to increase in an era of high interest rates.[86] Investors and speculators may already have seen through the "money illusion" of monetarists who seek to use an implicit neo-mercantilist strategy of controlling inflation and monetary policy in democratic societies with fairly independent central banks: They have put their money in the Euro and Xeno markets where inflation and international controls are even less likely to be effective. Central banks may well be more powerless than they appear and proposals to establish an international central bank to counter global inflation, while increasingly important for global adjustment, are apt to remain utopian unless the world debt crisis frightens Western Maintenance Men into entrepreneurial, international innovation.

If the underlying inflation rate in leading OECD countries such as the U.S. cannot be kept down by mere demand management, nor TIP policies, as appears likely given the dependence of this rate upon exogenous factors such as oil prices and the liquidity of Euromarkets, and if international controls of liquidity appear to be politically unfeasible, the optimum strategy for these nations appears to be a shift towards rewarding Entrepreneurship (and hence productivity increases) even at the risk of some Maintenance security. To some extent this is a call for a return to the old locomotive concept (of the U.S., West Germany, etc. leading the way in a global economic recovery) on the grounds that it was never really tried, not on the assumption that it alone can revive the world economy. For an implicit or explicit anti-locomotive policy appears perverse in terms of stimulating economic growth and is apt to prolong stagflation and postindustrial stalemate, mortgaging the future of the young for the Maintenance of the old. The focus of the future should be more upon growth stimulation than inflation fighting, upon employing the young rather than securing the old, upon supporting research and development rather than lame-duck industrial sectors and protective tariffs. Such an Entrepreneurial emphasis is particularly important in Europe where in many cases the "risk-free Western state" has cushioned those who are old or weak with adequate welfare, pension and health programs, including at least partial cost-of-living indexes that must be paid for by future economic growth. In contrast, the United States must aim for a balance between socio-economic needs of the elderly, sick and fixed-income groups not adequately covered by insurance and the counter needs for social and industrial restructuring to stimulate young entrepreneurs, increase productivity and make large, pampered industries more competitive. The Reagan administration has done neither, shoring up big business at the competitive expense of the small entrepreneur upon whom long-term economic dynamism and productivity ultimately depend in the American democratic system. The ascendancy of the monetarists in Western democracies is further apt to consolidate the position of the well-to-do without opening up a greater proportion of opportunities for the majority down the social ladder due to the moderate growth rates of the 1980s. For whereas inflation redistributes and mobilizes, anti-inflation policy recesses and freezes. Benefactors of the neoconservative trend in Great Britain, the United States, Australia and elsewhere in the First World are apt to interpret the boot-strap theory of helping the less advantaged more in terms of the boot than the strap.

The inflationary disease may be better than any feasible cure on the horizon promising to kill inflation once and for all, despite the clear social, economic and moral costs it entails. Democracy seems to lose either way, not to mention the less-developed countries who will continue to call for a New International Economic Order from the sidelines as the OECD (and OPEC) nations speed up their life-styles without necessarily improving the quality of life and worry about their own Maintenance more than about future generations or about international equity.

FOOTNOTES - PART III

1. The working definition of inflation used here is that of George L. Bach: "Inflation is a rise in the price level, or (what is the same thing) a fall in the purchasing power of the monetary unit." (G.S. Bach, The New Inflation; Providence, R.I.: Brown U. Press, 1972, pp. 5-6).

2. See Fred Hirsh, Social Limits to Growth (London: Routledge Kegan Paul, 1978). According to Hirsh, "The positional economy ... relates to all aspects of goods, services, work positions, and other social relationships that are either (1) scarce in some absolute or socially imposed sense or (2) subject to congestion or crowding through more extensive use." (p. 27)

3. See Gary Becker, "A Theory of the Allocation of Time," Economic Journal (September, 1965), p. 508; and Staffan B. Linder, The Harried Leisure Class (New York: Columbia University Press, 1970).

4. Hirsh, pp. 72-79.

5. See Max Weber, Wirtschaft und Gesellschaft (Tübingen, 1956), p. 20; and Ralf Dahrendorf, Lebenschancen (Frankfurt: Suhrkamp, 1979), pp. 48-50.

6. Weber's perceptions, in this context, appear not accidentally to be associated with the pessimistic psychology of Sigmund Freud (Freud, Civilization and Its Discontents, 1930), whereas Dahrendorf's correlate to a greater extent with the optimistic psychology of Abraham Maslow (see Maslow, Motivation and Personality, 1954).

7. In a 1980 year-end prognosis on West German television, Dahrendorf's view seemed to shift towards the neo-conservative trend in his call for belt-tightening and lower expectations. Another liberal gone neo-conservative, Whole Earth Catalog editor Stewart Brand, argued similarly late in 1980 that "Living below your means is a cheap way to be rich." But such a maxim may not pay off in an environment of high inflation that punishes savers and can turn them rapidly into defeatists.

8. Washington Post poll results as cited in Barry Sussman, "Inflation Concern Affects U.S.

Campaign," *International Herald Tribune*, April 22, 1980.

9. Union Bank of Switzerland, *Social Security in Ten Industrial Nations* (Zurich: Economic Research Department of Union Bank of Switzerland, 1977), p. 7.

10. See, for example, "Inflation is Wrecking the Private Pension System," in *Business Week*, May 12, 1980, pp. 92-99.

11. "Inflation's COLA Cure," *Time*, July 28, 1980, p. 45.

12. *Business Week*, May 12, 1980, p. 94.

13. *Ibid*., pp. 94-95.

14. In theory, these are mutually exclusive (but non-exhaustive) types of inflation strategies. In practice, it is the mixture or specific cluster of types that distinguishes different individuals, firms and states. No doubt quantitative theorists could easily create ordinal scales for weighing (or measuring) the extent of the existence of any one type compared to others in a specific case or comparison. Here it is posited that the mix of Maintenance and Entrepreneurial types is the most fruitful combination for future productivity and anti-inflation effectiveness.

15. Peter Marris, *Loss and Change* (New York: Pantheon, 1974), pp. 114-116.

16. Robert Heilbroner, "The Inflation in Your Future," *The New York Review of Books*, Vol. XXVII, No. 7, May 1, 1980, p. 7.

17. *Ibid*., p. 7.

18. Figures from a study of the Mortgage Bankers Association of America, as reported in John B. Willman, "Report Affirms Worth of Real Estate," *International Herald Tribune*, July 8, 1980. For the 1981-82 decline in the rate of housing depreciation, see *The New York Times*, November 16, 1981 and December 5, 1982 ("Business").

19. *Ibid*.

20. The discussion that follows concerning retired people is based on the U.S. situation and is not

directly applicable in most cases to European countries, where pension and welfare systems are usually indexed to inflation and where almost all citizens are eligible for such benefits. On the other hand, recent American financial innovations, such as the widespread use of money market funds, may well become increasingly relevant for the Europeans who watch the loss of purchasing power in their bank deposits and other family-owned financial assets and whose traditional patterns of expenditure and consumption are threatened by prices they can no longer afford.

21. "The Death of Equities: How Inflation Is Destroying the Stock Market," Business Week, August 13, 1979, p. 54.

22. See William D. Nordhaus, "The Falling Share of Profits," in Brookings Papers on Economic Activity, Vol. 1, edited by Arthus M. Okun and George L. Perry; (Washington, D.C.: The Brookings Institution, 1974), pp. 169-208.

23. "The Death of Equities," p. 54.

24. See Jason Epstein, "Capitalism and Socialism: Declining Returns," The New York Review of Books, February 17, 1977.

25. "The Death of Equities," p. 54.

26. "Inflation is Wrecking the Private Pension System," p. 92.

27. Peter F. Drucker, The Unseen Revolution: How Pension Fund Socialism Came to America. (New York: Harper and Row, 1977).

28. Mancur Olson, The Logic of Collective Action: Public Goods and the Theory of Groups (Cambridge, Mass.: Harvard University Press, 1971).

29. These comparisons are based upon compound appreciation between 1972 and 1979. See "The Death of Equities," p. 56.

30. Jean Ross-Skinner, "Art: How Good an Investment?," Dun's Review, May 1980, pp. 60-68.

31. "How to Play the Business Cycle," Business

Week, June 9, 1980, p. 117. Also see W.W. Rostow, *Why the Poor Get Richer and the Rich Slow Down* (Austin: University of Texas Press, 1980), Chapters 1-2.

32. "Investing for the Recession and Beyond," *Business Week*, June 9, 1980, pp. 114-115. Also see R. Isaak, "Inflation Strategies in the 1980's," *Adherent*, Vol. 9, No. 1, March 1982.

33. U.S. Department of Labor statistics as reported in Robert A. Rosenblatt, "The Moderate Life in U.S. Now Costs $20,000 a Year," *The International Herald Tribune*, May 2, 1980.

34. Olson, p. 2.

35. See "Objectives," in Robert Townsend, *Up the Organization: How to Stop the Corporation from Stifling People and Strangling Profits* (London: Michael Joseph Ltd., 1970), pp. 120-121. Also see Peter Drucker, *Managing for Results* (New York: Harper and Row, 1964), and especially Ruth Mack, *Planning on Uncertainty* (New York: John Wiley, 1971), Chapters 8 and 12 on "the conservative bias."

36. As cited in "The New Planning," *Business Week*, December 18, 1978, p. 62.

37. This low inflation era of the 1950s and 1960s may well ease time distortions in comparisons across decades, hiding entrepreneurial behavior and initiatives due to a time lag that must pass before their results show through. But companies without such innovative "jack-in-the-boxes" beneath the surface may have to consider radical restructuring and new strategies to survive the inflationary 1980s. Of course, an opposite kind of time distortion may occur: Inflationary periods may hide entrepreneurial failures for a longer time than in periods of near-price stability.

38. *Ibid.*, p. 62.

39. William C. Norris, "A Risk-Avoiding, Selfish Society," *Business Week*, January 28, 1980, p. 20.

40. See Joseph H. Schumpeter, *Capitalism, Socialism and Democracy* (New York: Harper and Row, 1950), 3rd edition, Chapter XII.

41. See Alfred Rappaport, "Measuring Company Growth Capacity During Inflation," *Harvard Business Review*, Jan.-Feb. 1979, pp. 91-100; Gerald R. Rosen, "The CPI Controversy," *Dun's Review*, May 1980, pp. 54-57; and "Which Inflation Rate Should Business Use," *Business Week*, April 7, 1980, pp. 94-97.

42. Winston Williams, "U.S. Capital Outlays Seen at Cyclical Peak," *International Herald Tribune*, May 28, 1980.

43. "Hard Times for Big Business?" *Newsweek*, May 26, 1980, p. 37.

44. *Ibid*. Also see "Inflation Props Up Profits," *Business Week*, May 19, 1980.

45. "The Death of Equities," p. 56.

46. "Merrill Lynch's Marauding Herd," *Time*, August 4, 1980, p. 47.

47. "Hot Seller: Bonds Indexed to Oil and Gold," *Business Week*, August 13, 1979, p. 74.

48. "U.S. Investors May Diversify Overseas," *International Herald Tribune*, May 17-18, 1980.

49. See: Lewis D. Solomon, *Multinational Corporations and the Emerging World Order* (Port Washington, New York: Kennikat Press, 1978), Chapter 3.

50. See C.F. Bergsten, Thomas Horst and Theodore Moran, *American Multinationals and American Interests* (Washington, D.C.: Brookings Institute, 1978), Chapter 7.

51. Yair Aharoni, *The Foreign Investment Decision Process* (Cambridge, Massachusetts: Harvard University Press, Graduate School of Business Administration, 1966), pp. 115-116.

52. Brandt Commission, *North-South: A Program for Survival* (Cambridge, Mass.: The MIT Press, 1980), pp. 187-188.

53. See "*La Mistica dell'Inflazione*," Chapter 9 in Vittorio Mathieu, *Cancro in Occidente: Le rovine del giacobinismo* (Milano: Editorale Nuova, 1980).

54. M.D.K.W. Foot, "Monetary Targets: Their Nature and Record in the Major Economics," presented at the City of London University, May 1979.

55. M.S. Mendelsohn, "Beating Inflation: The German and Swiss Experience," The Banker, December 1979.

56. OECD figures for 1979 as cited in "U.S. Retreats to 9th Place in OECD List," The International Herald Tribune, April 25, 1980.

Of course, 1979 data biased U.S. national income downwards in international comparisons based on actual exchange rates (as in the case of OECD data here); nevertheless, the data serve to highlight the point being made--that Switzerland and West Germany are rich countries.

57. See, for example, "West Germany: A Social Market Economy," Chapter Two in R. Isaak, European Politics: Political Economy and Policy Making in Western Democracies (New York: St. Martin's Press, 1980).

58. As M.S. Mendelsohn notes: "Both were ... in the exceptional position of being able to run down their imported labour by a net 25 per cent after 1974, although they now have correspondingly less scope than five years ago for disinflation at other people's expense." In: "Beating Inflation: The German and Swiss Experience," p. 37. Also see The German Tribune, No. 1029, March 21, 1982.

59. Ibid., p. 38.

60. Stanley W. Black, Floating Exchange Rates and National Economic Policy (New Haven: Yale University Press, 1977), pp. 98-99.

61. Mendelsohn, p. 39.

62. Deutsches Institut für Wirtschaftsforschung, Wochenbericht 22/76, p. 224.

63. See "Labor-Management Codetermination or Industrial Democracy," in R. Isaak, European Politics, pp. 55-56.

64. As cited in "Some Interest Rate Toulette," Time, July 28, 1980, p. 44. On the relationship

between interest rates and anticipated inflation, see the articles in the debate in the American Economic Review, June and September 1982.

65. Karen W. Arenson, "New Storm Gathering in Interest Rates?: A Stubborn Cycle Points to Higher Levels," New York Times, August 3, 1980.

66. See William D. Nordhaus, "The Political Business Cycle," Review of Economic Studies, 42, 1975.

67. See "Will the New Pay Guide Cut Prices Loose?," Business Week, February 4, 1980, pp. 28-29, and Jill Wechsler, "COWPS Eyes Prices," Dun's Review, May 1980, p. 99.

68. For details on TIP see Sidney Weintraub, "Proposal for an Anti-Inflation Package," Challenge, September-October 1978, pp. 53-54; and Sidney Weintraub, Capitalism's Inflation and Unemployment Crisis (Reading, Massachusetts: Addison-Wesley Publishing Company, 1978), Part III, pp. 113-164.

69. See Ann W. Reilly, "The Battle Among Conservatives," Dun's Review, May 1980, pp. 48-53; and Gardner Ackley, "Increased Inflation: A Harbinger of Fear in the Business Community?" same issue, p. 11.

70. Murray Seeger, "Iceland Fishing for Million-Kronur Inflation Answer," International Herald Tribune, Tuesday, July 8, 1980, p. 4.

71. See R. Isaak, "The Individual in International Politics: Solving the Level-of-Analysis Problem," Polity, 7, No. 2 (1974); and Ralph P. Hummel, "Notes on Reification of Inflation and a Possible Phenomenological Reduction," Urbia Associates Occasional Papers Series, Phen. 1980-2 (Spruce Head Island, Maine: mimeographed, 1980).

72. See European Politics, especially pp. 2-24 and following. Also see Peter Katzenstein, ed., Between Power and Plenty (Madison, Wisconsin: The University of Wisconsin Press, 1978).

73. Ibid., "Great Britain: A Socialized Economy in Crisis," pp. 99-125. For the rationale of the British workers see John H. Goldthorpe's perceptive essay "The Current Inflation: Towards a Sociological

Account," in The Political Economy of Inflation, edited by Fred Hirsch and J. Goldthorpe (Cambridge, Massachusetts: Harvard University Press, 1978), pp. 186-214.

74. Marian Bond, "Exchange Rates, Inflation and the Vicious Circle," Finance and Development, March 1980, p. 30. Also see John Cornwall, Modern Capitalism (Oxford: Martin Robertson, 1977) and Otto Eckstein, Core Inflation (Englewood Cliffs, N.J.: Prentice-Hall, 1982).

75. Ibid.

76. Ibid.

77. Thus, the 1979 Tokyo Round of Multilateral Trade Negotiations of the developed countries on tariff reductions deterred the creeping protectionism of the mid-1970s and benefited the exports of the developing countries; codes on non-tariff restrictions were developed, but of the developing countries only Argentina subscribed and benefits from them. See Bela Balassa, "The Tokyo Round and the Developing Countries," Journal of World Trade Law, Vol. 14, No. 2, March-April 1980, pp. 93-118; and Andrew Shonfield, "The Politics of the Mixed Economy in the International System of the 1970s," International Affairs, Vol. 56, Jan. 1980, No. 1, pp. 1-14. Also see William Cline et al., World Inflation and the Developing Countries (Washington, D.C.: Brookings, 1981) and Richard Medley, ed., The Politics of Inflation (New York: Pergamon, 1982).

78. My interpretation here of the reactions of OECD countries to inflation is indebted to Marshall Cass, American Economic Policy Advisor to the OECD, who spoke on positive adjustment at the OECD, Paris on February 15, 1980.

79. Wilhelm Hankel, "Germany: Economic Nationalism in the International Economy," in Wilfrid L. Kohl and Giorgio Basevi (eds), West Germany: A European and Global Power (Lexington, Mass.: D.C. Heath and Co., 1980), pp. 21-43.

80. W. Hankel, Prosperity Amidst Crisis: Austria's Economic Policy and the Energy Crunch (Boulder, Colorado: Westview Press, 1980), p. 149.

81. See "The Political Economy of the European Monetary System: A Conference Report," edited by Giorgio Basevi and Wilfrid L. Kohl, Occasional Paper No. 31, June 1980 (Bologna, Italy: The Johns Hopkins University Bologna Center).

82. See Paul Lewis, "EEC Acts to Extend Monetary System, Promote Ecu," International Herald Tribune, December 4, 1980.

83. See Tom de Vries, "On the Meaning and Future of the European Monetary System," Essays in International Finance, No. 138, September 1980 (Department of Economics, Princeton University, Princeton, New Jersey); and R. Isaak, European Politics, pp. 179-201.

84. F. Harvey Popell, "How Inflation Undermines Morality," Business Week, May 5, 1980, p. 20.

85. Leonard Silk, "Web of Inflation Growing More Tangled," International Herald Tribune, December 4, 1980. Also see Ralph Bryant, Money and Monetary Policy in Interdependent Nations (Washington, D.C.: Brookings, 1980).

86. For example, see John A. Davenport, "A Testing Time for Monetarism," Fortune, October 6, 1980.

PART IV

THESES AND COMMENTARY OF INTERNATIONAL INFLATION WORKSHOP, APRIL 29-30, 1981 AT JOHNS HOPKINS SAIS BOLOGNA CENTER, BOLOGNA, ITALY

Theses and Commentary of International Workshop
April 29-30, 1981 at SAIS Bologna Center

Wilhelm Hankel's Theses:
"Modern Inflation - Rationale, Background, Illusions"

Robert Isaak's Theses:
"Modern Anti-Inflation Strategies - Private and Public; or, Survival Lessons from the 1970s"

Karl Deutsch, Chairman:
Professor of Government of Harvard University and Director of The Science Center in Berlin

Commentators:

Stephen Goldfeld, Professor of Economics and Chairman of Department of Economics at Princeton University and Member of the Council of Economic Advisors in Carter Administration

David Coe, Economist at the Organization for Economic Cooperation and Development, Paris

Wolfgang Hager, professorial research associate of the European University Institute, Florence

Edward Weisband, Professor of Political Science at the State University of New York at Binghamton, New York

Ahmet Aker, Associate Professor of Economics at The Johns Hopkins University, SAIS

Stefano Zamagni, Professor of Economics at the University of Bologna and Visiting Professor of Economics at The Johns Hopkins University, SAIS

Vera Zamagni, Professor of Economic History at the University of Florence and Visiting Professor of The Johns Hopkins University, SAIS

Wilhelm Hankel's Theses:

Modern Inflation - Rationale, Background, Illusions

I.

Although one of history's oldest recorded economic diseases, inflation has been ignored for a long time by professionals concerned with political economy. Economists, playing the role of political barristers in public affairs, protested against the scarcity of money (Mercantilists), state controls and monopolies in economic life (Classicists), and the mystical belief in the optimal guidance of laissez-faire (Marx as well as Keynes--the former against its social consequences, the latter against its employment performance), yet for centuries they never protested against the freedom of prices to increase. Only in exceptional times of hyper-inflation did they plead against the "usury" by prices.

Although political economy started some 300 years ago with Jean Bodin's famous explanation of (and attack on) Spanish-imported inflation his followers were preoccupied with other topics: external surpluses, economic growth and distribution, price determination, partial and general equilibrium conditions, employment and international order questions--problems regarded to be of much higher priority than the continuation of inflation.

II.

Why has inflation become a key issue of public debate and policy after World War II and especially since the end of the Golden Fifties, with growing intellectual self-acceleration? What is behind the new and astonishing conformity of traditionally controversial political camps: the schools of Neo-classicists, Neo-Keynesians as well as Neo-Marxians? For they all are in agreement that inflation is the arch enemy of:

- functioning market economies, disturbing the selection mechanism of prices;
- fair income and wealth distribution, dividing society into involuntary inflation losers and unearned inflation winners;

- full absorption of available resources, producing all the negative effects of stagflation.

When all economic doctrines seem to revel in harmony then the church may approach a new condition of unification, but a new state of dogmatism too.

III.

At least two facts behind this new and untypical anti-inflation bias of modern economic thinking are worth some reflection: First, the forgotten (or repressed) lesson of the twin fathers of modern economic growth theory: the Swedish economist Knut Wicksell and the Austro-American economist Joseph A. Schumpeter. Wicksell made clear that there is no economic growth without inflationary credit-financing of real investments; Schumpeter that there is no chance for any positive saving reward, a positive real interest rate in the economy, without the risky job of dynamic innovators using their free access to credit markets to fill the gap between needed investments and available saving. Second, the coincidence of our present crusade against inflation with a period of not only relatively mild inflation compared with previous times and events, but also with a stage of societal development, where people have learned to survive with inflation much better than ever in history. If this generation of money users is living in better conditions (in terms of both income payments as well as wealth storing) than any other generation before, we have to ask: Is this despite or because of inflation? And why are the chances to prevent unwanted consequences of redistribution by inflation more highly sophisticated than ever in societal development?

That is why we have to ask what the factors are behind this new consensus that inflation has to be exorcised: "Inflationem esse delendam." And why has this to be done by public actions instead of private self-protection as people were motivated to do in all previous times, when privacy in benefit-maximizing as well as in cost- and risk-minimizing was taken for granted.

Since this second point is analyzed in Robert Isaak's theses to follow concerning private anti-inflation strategies and reactions, I will concentrate on the first point: Why have we forgotten or repressed obvious lessons from earlier stages and understandings of the subject?

IV.

Inflation in all times and societies has been politically tolerated as a distribution struggle between old owners of resources (land, means of production) and their new challengers--a graceless fight, in which money was the powder and exploding prices the bullets undermining the bastions of traditional proprietorship. And curiously enough, for centuries people accepted this permanent deprivation (or exploitation) via rising prices. Instead of this people reacted sensitively against rising taxes (which compared with rates of today were ridiculously low). The great democratic revolutions of the 17th and 18th centuries (in England, U.S.A., France) were tax- not anti-inflation strikes: No taxation without representation; but not yet: No political mercy for governments benignly neglecting the usury of prices--regardless from where it comes and whether or not there are instruments available to reduce it to tolerable limits!

The inflation tolerance if not robustness of earlier capitalistic as well as acquisitive societies cannot be explained by ignoring the impact between the available volume of money for spending and the trend in prices. For economists and societies of those times were at least as modern as the majority of Monetarists of today, using the same--but minimally refined--Quantitative Theory of Money! If inflation had been regarded as a political challenge to those societies their economists would not have hesitated to enlighten princes as well as people about the very nature and consequences of rising price levels. Yet, this enlightenment had no demand, because princes and peoples accepted tacitly or unconsciously the prevailing rate of inflation. And why? The young bourgeoisie of the *ancien-regime* society was primarily motivated to expropriate the old owners of resources, the privileged nobility. And the threatened nobility, on the other side, was either blind or indifferent to this new challenge of new competitors for their old privileges: *apres nous le deluge*. Wealthy classes of the *ancien regime* felt protected against the dangers of inflation either by arrogance or because the bulk of their wealth was invested in real estate and appreciated more or less in line with the prevailing inflation rates. Thus, inflation was for the under classes the vehicle lifting them up to higher and wealthier levels of the social pyramid and for the upper classes no drop downwards, at least in their own self-conception. Although confronted in reality with the challenge of social decline they failed to feel so.

V.

Yet, in the nouveau-regime societies of our rich and egalitarian mass wealth and welfare-states things have changed completely: the social pyramid is becoming transformed into a social cylinder, having only a short pike of "abnormal" high income and wealth nobility. And much more important: the biggest part and share of the newly formed social cylinder--acquired (earned and accumulated) mass wealth and welfare--is held in the form of non-risk-sharing, yield-bearing money assets: bonds, certificates, bank accounts, insurance policies, etc. This newly piled up money wealth is the credit equivalent of the debt-financed real investments of the entrepreneurial and the public sector. So private households and, as mediaries, banks and insurance companies are becoming the main creditors (or financers) of the real capital formation within the economy--whereas entrepreneurial and public sectors still remain the main debtors (or investors) in modern societies.

The consequences of such a split society in which the "money asset" side of the wealth cylinder is representing saver interests and mentality the other "real asset" side investors' interests and mentality in terms of inflation reactions are self-evident: any percentage of annual inflation means a relative real loss on (money) capital account, damaging the savers (private households as well as financial institutions) and benefiting the debtors (investing entrepreneurs as well as the deficit-making public sector). If the inflation rate is exceeding the nominal yields of money assets of the saving sectors within the economy, relative real losses on capital account will turn over to absolute real losses for savers and absolute real profits for debtors: an inflation-driven redistribution of the existing wealth structure.

Or to demonstrate this in terms of income-capital-relations: Given the amounts of money assets held by private households and powerful financial institutions (banks and insurance companies) each percentage of annual inflation that is damaging those sectors harder than they can improve their current (nominal) income by one percent wage or profit increase!

However, the losses on saver's accounts are financing the unexpected inflationary windfall profits on investor's accounts and the question arises: Why is this class of potential inflation winners in any society no longer in favor of more instead of less inflation in the economy? The answer simply is given by the democratic voting power system: one man one vote. Since in any mass wealth and welfare society the number (and therefore voting power) of savers and potential savers by far exceeds the number of real asset holders (investors) whose fortunes are moreover concentrated in the hands and on account of a minority, this type of society seems to be much more governed by savers' interests and the savers' mentality than (as in the old structured societies) by those of debt-financed investors.

Thus, the predominance of the savers' mentality over the investors' mentality, which is a characteristic feature of all rich, egalitarian democracies, seems to be the price we have to pay not only for social progress, the welfare of masses, but for political progress too: the successful banishing of plutocratic elements in the voting system (so many dollars--so many votes) via a pure democratic system (so many heads--so many votes). In modern mass welfare and democratic societies inflation, therefore, has changed its social function: It no longer uplifts poor and productive classes to the top of pyramids; on the contrary, it confronts all savers and money-asset holders of the new wealth cylinder (a majority of the constituency) with unwanted losses and social decline.

In this new wealth structure and political climate of a society in which money has become the main store of wealth for people working as employees instead of employers (or entrepreneurs), the old patterns and frontiers of the traditional class interests and struggles tend to disappear. Class conflict is becoming increasingly substituted for by a new class solidarity and social contract among potential inflation losers. All money wealth holders independent from the absolute size of their fortunes have something to lose from inflation: with their fortunes go also their social standing and security.

This is why inflation and its taming has become the aim of a social crusade. This is why modern Monetarism, which started as an obscure sect of economic dissidents, could climb up to the position of a generally accepted conservative orthodoxy maintaining that inflation--against all historical evidence--no longer solves any problem: neither correcting unwanted unemployment nor socially unwanted distribution and that benign neglect in terms of inflation is the hardcore of all new and ungovernable social conflicts: of unemployment, unrest, disintegration in and between societies.

Yet how convincing is this new, conservative philosophy? And much more specifically: why are the existing groups of at least potential winners of inflation (entrepreneurs and those of the public sector) not in opposition to this clear-cut savers' mentality-inspired concept?

VI.

Modern Monetarism, perceived to free the modern society from all types of "money illusion" (the illusion that money as value-unit for income and wealth evaluation has no longer the function of a metric yardstick), is replacing one illusion about money by three other illusions about inflation:

<u>The First Illusion</u>: Inflation is an illness but not the normal condition of any money as well as credit as a means for mobilizing resources and financing society; therefore, a growing and permanently restructuring society has not the choice of <u>if</u> it can afford inflation, but only <u>how much</u>. The problem of those societies is not to compare the costs of inflation (in terms of savers' losses) with regard to a distribution of wealth fixed forever, which as a "goal" always is assumed to have a positive value, but to measure the opportunity costs of non-inflation or price-level stability (in terms of real growth, productivity and innovation losses) and those of inflation (in terms of the political indignance of inflation-damaged groups) and to find the diagonal in the parallelogram of all those forces, in the form of a societal minimal cost combination, providing the society with sufficient growth, productivity innovation and social stability.

The Second Illusion: The attempt of all social groups to fix "their" traditional share of real income and wealth (via agreements in real instead of nominal bargaining terms, real wages, real interests, etc.) is neither eliminating inflation nor its undesired (negative) distribution consequences. On the contrary, inflation as well as its by-product, redistribution, will only be fueled by such status-quo fixing actions. The advocates of any real bargaining strategy (whether in the form of real calculations, indexations, etc.) fail to recognize the paradox (of survival law) or any society vested with different degrees of market power (from monopoly to competition) and endowed with an imperfect money constitution. For in such a society the more powerful (or monopolistic) sectors have the advantage of anticipating, if not realizing, their own inflation expectations (if not inflation claims) successfully, whereas the weaker and less credit-worthy (or competitive) sectors miss this chance. Small business, therefore, is not "beautiful" but suffers much more under anti-inflation policies than under inflation. (Compare the robustness of big and multinational enterprises, determining their own cash flow and self-financing via price setting versus the small and national enterprises, which are dependent upon the availability and costs of credit financing).

Thus, the traditional anti-inflation policy via scarcity of money supply and high nominal interest rates (which covers in reality only the "national" segments of the "ubiqious" world-wide offers of money and credit) is decimating the price- and credit- (competitive) sectors of any economy and strengthening indirectly but effectively the market position and weight of the inflation-resistant monopolistic sectors. That is why big business unanimously is in favor of hard currency policy: it annihilates weaker competitors and improves their own chances, but at the price of a higher degree of monopoly and therefore resistance against inflation as well as traditional anti-inflation policies in society as a whole.

The Third Illusion: A public guarantee for protection, if not prevention of inflation (a promise which can't be kept) is improving instead of undermining the cohesion of democratic societies. If it becomes evident that inflation with its by-product of unwanted redistribution cannot be controlled as promised, voters will accuse the system first of being "ungovernable" and later of being "unreliable" and will begin to sympathize with a nostalgic longing for "strong," "conservative" and perhaps "less democratic" government. For the failure of anti-inflation policy enforces not only the dangers of social decline and painful losses of positional goods for entire groups; it also damages the individual actor who, trusting the public inflation protection, has insured his "private" possibilities to protect himself against the erosion of his position due to inflation.

Thus, the official fight against inflation, using inadequate instruments (namely anti-competition instead of anti-monopoly measures and national instead of international money controls) is not only counter-productive: strengthening instead of correcting the monopolistic background of stagflation in society, this position is over-challenging the democratic society with an aim which could not be fulfilled, neither in the past nor (as it seems) in the future (namely freedom from inflation).

VII.

The old class struggle which in modern mass wealth and welfare societies is buried because the real capital formation of the proprietors of the means of production (the entrepreneurial class) is matched and financed by a still growing money capital formation of non-entrepreneurial households as well as financial institutions (banks and insurance companies) has shifted over to two other levels: <u>within</u> society to the relation between the "younger" generation still working and the "older" generation no longer working, and <u>among</u> societies to the relation between the "rich" nations of the North and the "poor" nations of the South of the same globe. The old class conflict about resources and their distribution is now on the verge of continuing in the form of a new generation conflict between youngsters and oldsters of the same society; and world trade as a competitive struggle of nations for more favorable terms of trade is becoming a strong distribution struggle about the share and pricing of world resources, whereby terms of trade are no longer regarded as market but as political parameters.

In Western societies the transfer burden for the oldsters is growing due to changes in the human and economic life-cycles: older people are living longer after retiring, enjoying a second (generation) life after the end of their working life; younger and still active people are (at least for the coming generation) declining in their demographic share and weight: in order to aliment the oldsters they have to work with higher productivity or less disposable income (after deduction of their social generation tax). The huge and growing deficits of social security systems (so alarming in the Federal Republic of Germany) signal not only a future distribution struggle between old and young, but also the incompetence of "weak" democratic governments to finance this unavoidable inter-generation transfer <u>openly</u>, i.e. via taxes instead of inflation. Given the demographic structures and trends (the number and individual living conditions of the oldsters without any "formula" of more or less dynamic pension calculations as well as the growth thereafter of younger people whose employment and productivity still is uncertain) in nearly all Western societies the real income share of oldsters at the end of the century is approaching the critical mark of 50% of the disposable gross per-capita income of the young and working people! The question arises: how can this survival problem of Western society and culture be financed without the redistribution help of inflation?

Perhaps more clearly than anywhere else, the mismanagement (if not dishonesty) of any anti-inflation guarantee here becomes manifest. For the politically built-in inflation break would kill a big part of the employment needed as well as the productivity of younger working generations in order to aliment and to finance the real income of the oldsters. Anti-inflation policies, therefore, not only tend to accelerate the generation conflict; they constitute a peril for each generation contract, because the economic well-being of the older people is assured by the earnings of the younger people--one of the indispensable foundations of a human society and its continuation. For if one generation rejects life-support for the previous generation the following generation will do the same to the present young generation, if it becomes old and inactive.

The strong anti-inflation bias of northern industrialized countries is also aggravating the conflict potential of the "underdeveloped" countries of the South. LDCs which imitate the status-quo policies of the richer countries or are forced to do so through pressures from supranational Development-

Aid- organizations (as the World Bank, I.M.F. and Western creditor-clubs) not only sacrifice possible development, growth and catch-up chances, they endanger their internal dynamism by these stability-first strategies. Their models for self-help and self-development, as well as reducing their dependence from resource-transfer from the North, therefore, should be derived not from our present and modern societal and economic doctrines but from our past--when the now developed First World was much nearer to the status of the still lesser developed countries of today.

Especially here the Western "block-floating" of foreign exchange rates, allowing differentials in national degrees and rhythm of inflation, is applicable: to give low-productivity LDCs a fair competitive chance on world markets. Then the structurally higher inflation rate of LDCs could (and would) be compensated for by the higher competitiveness of their foreign prices and terms of trade due to weaker but more realistic foreign exchange rates.

VIII.

In summary, inflation is more a part of the life-cycle of growing and renewing societies than its biased challengers observe. If societies are young and poor and are governed by elites defending their traditionally inherited (feudalistic) proprietorships the inflationary financed evolution (which is nothing else than the economic expropriation of the privileged old owners of resources) replaces the otherwise unavoidable revolution. The old nobility has only the choice of adjusting or declining. As societies become old and rich they have to resist the socially and politically understandable illusion that inflation can be exorcised; for their status-quo can never be regarded as a "streetcar named desire." They still need inflation in order to master unavoidable challenges of the future, which require a higher degree of flexibility of society and government than can be assumed to exist normally in wealthy and welfare democracies. Examples of this kind are the still unsolved problems of inner-social generation and inter-societal development conflicts.

Thus, inflation is by its nature and consequences simultaneously both "challenge" and "response." Resulting from the oldest source in economic progress:

the productivity in money production and its permanent decreasing costs which liberate blocked real resources for more, newer and higher productive real investments; inflation is not only an indispensable vehicle for social progress, it contains a built-in tendency for self-correction--but only in cases in which the mobilized resources were used to finance productive innovations rather than unproductive wars, prestigious state projects and private and public luxury.

In the process of mankind's social development inflation plays a role similar to that of Mephisto in the story of Dr. Faust: it is as a part of worldly energy pretending the bad which ultimately creates the good.

And how can the individual protect himself in this risky inflationary environment? This is the topic treated in the following analysis by Robert Isaak.

Robert Isaak's Theses:

Modern Anti-Inflation Strategies - Private and Public
or
Survival Lessons from the 1970s

In late September of 1980 a stranger in his late 20s walked into the casino at Binion's Horseshoe Club in Las Vegas carrying two suitcases. One was empty, while the other contained $777,000 in cash. Jack Binion, the cashier, approved the conversion of the cash into chips, which the stranger took to the craps table. He put all of them on the "Don't Pass" line--an even-money bet that the woman rolling the dice wouldn't make her point. She rolled the dice and lost. The stranger calmly left the table, cashed in his chips, split the $1,554,000 between the two suitcases and said to the cashier as he left the casino: "You know, this damned inflation was just eroding the money. I figured I might as well double it or lose it."

I.

From the viewpoint of the individual, inflation implies the constant threat of the loss of value over time. Anti-inflation strategies and policies stem basically from this fear of loss, a fear of the depreciation of value, status and living standards in advanced Western democracies.

Sociologist Peter Marris showed that when people experience intense change or loss, they revert to a conservative psychological impulse, seeking to restore old patterns and values. Social scarcity has compounded the sense of material privation in the competition for positional goods and services; the resulting threat of lower living standards and underemployment makes it seem as if everyone has less time to spend less real income.

Time economists such as Gary Becker and Staffan Linder have demonstrated the tendency for greater affluence to make modern man more harried rather than less. Time becomes scarcer as the output of material goods increases while the time in which to use them remains constant. Two consequences result that inflation serves only to intensify: the individual needs additional time for consumption and additional income to maintain his or her position in society.

The financial pressures of modern inflation upon the myth of self-sufficiency in Western societies resulted in a widespread conservative psychological reaction in the 1970s, with inflation paradoxically serving to stimulate the Western logic of maximizing individual interest while simultaneously undermining the collective conditions that make self-sufficiency possible. The consequence has been the extension of particularistic Olsonian democracy *ad absurdum*.

II.

At least four typical patterns of Weberian "ideal types" of individual strategies aimed at coping with inflationary change can be identified and compared in terms of risk orientation, time horizon, guiding motive, consumption pattern and characteristic portfolio mix:

(i) The Defeatist: takes as few risks as possible, cutting costs rather than risking assets; this type is past-oriented, passive, defensive and plagued by the fear of loss and a neurotic conservative impulse. The Defeatist is thrifty in consumption with a security-oriented, portfolio mix.

(ii) The Free Rider: takes high risks at no cost or low cost, specializing in living at someone else's expense; present-oriented, the Free Rider has active-passive motivation or *maximin*--maximizing individual gains and minimizing personal costs; this type is characterized by high individual consumption when others pay, low otherwise, and a portfolio mix centered on cheap money or upon debt at low interest rates.

(iii) The Maintenance Man: takes limited risks at moderate cost to keep up with the business cycle and inflation; he is a present-oriented, short-term realist guided by a passive-active motive who seeks to coopt change in order to insure stability; the Maintenance Man consumes high quality now before costs go even higher and his portfolio mix stresses stable returns, liquidity, diversity and flexibility.

(iv) The Entrepreneur: takes high risks even at high costs aiming to come out ahead of inflation; this type is characterized by aggressive motivation stemming from tension between perception of handicap and potential advantage, seeking to thrust all energy and resources in the direction of the highest probable pay-off. Future-oriented, the Entrepreneur has an all-or-nothing consumption pattern with a portfolio mix focused upon the highest return through astute gambles on the business cycle.

When these ideal types of inflation strategy are used as analytical categories they can be combined to describe typical reactions to the inflation of the 1970s focusing upon four levels of analysis: the Individual, the Corporate or Institutional, the State, and the International System.

(i) The Individual: Among passive individuals a class difference was consolidated between Vested Defeatists (owning a house or apartment) and Uninvested or Disinvested Defeatists (renters). Within the United States, for example, a dollar invested in a house in 1968 rose to 1.29 in purchasing power in 1978. During this decade, if the same dollar was kept in the owner's pocket it would have fallen to .53, if invested in a common stock it would have been worth .78, if held in a savings account worth .89, and if put in a corporate bond, up to 1.20--still less than housing appreciation. The single most important financial distinction between individuals in coping with inflation in the 1970s may well have been between those who owned a house at the beginning of the decade and those who did not.

In the past decade, given factors such as sharp real estate appreciation, inflation intensified conflict within socio-economic groups more than increasing social distance between them, moving everyone to run faster on the same escalator. After inflation and tax have been discounted, real incomes in the United States rose at almost the same rate during the inflationary years of 1972-1978 as during the boom years of 1966-1972. And when the curve of real per capita income did turn down in 1979, it seemed to have been due to government attempts to slow inflation by halting economic growth. The relative disadvantage of the poor, the blacks and the aged did not in general appear to become worse in this period, despite popular beliefs to the contrary. As economist Robert Heilbroner noted, "The distribution of the population on the steps of the national escalator has remained about the same, although the escalator itself has been moving faster."

Among individuals in the 1970s, those invested in real estate and hard assets won, those in stocks lost; those over 65 lost most in stocks. American stocks averaged a return of less than 3% through the decade of the 1970s, and in the first half of the decade the number of investors in stocks dropped in every age group but that of individuals 65 and older, whereas the number of investors in this older group went up by more than 30% largely due to the mismanagement of pension funds. Thus those retired on fixed incomes were hit hardest by the inflation of the 1970s, particularly in the United States.

The winners in the past inflationary decade were those who diversified investment in hard assets, that is, those who adopted a balance between the Maintenance Man and Entrepreneur strategies aimed at the concrete. During this period, stamps appreciated more consistently than almost anything else including gold, which came in a close second due to speculative swings in the buying and selling of this commodity. Diamonds and farmland ranked as steady gainers in the next category, followed by single-family houses. Significantly behind all these tangible assets came average appreciation through investment in foreign currencies and high-grade corporate bonds which more or less kept even with the rise in the Consumer Price Index (or CPI). Stocks, of course, trailed the CPI. And the prices of modern paintings, collectors' books and prints did a great deal better than equivalent stock market investments would have reaped. Furthermore, by constantly rolling over short-term paper investments in relatively secure sectors, such as Treasury Bills and municipal bonds, money-fund managers outpaced the returns on stocks and bonds by a considerable amount for their clients. Of course as interest rates fall, the astute Maintenance-Entrepreneur shifts his investment with the business cycle, perhaps into bonds where prices fall after short-term interest rates have peaked, perhaps indicating the beginning of a recession; the optimum strategist waits three or four months for them to bottom out and then perhaps buys energy-related, high technology or inflation-proof stocks (like beer and tobacco) as they start to move upward.

In summary, those most undermined by inflation in the 1970s were the unemployed, the poor and the old--people forced to become Defeatists or Free Riders by default; those who could afford the prerequisites coped best with inflation using a flexible balance between Maintenance and Entrepreneur strategies. After all, not just everyone could spend a record 31,000 dollars for an 1822 bottle of Chateau Lafite at a 1980 wine auction, as did restaurant owner John Grisanti in San Francisco. Unless the market incentives are changed in the future, as Robert Salomon of Saloman Brothers suggests: "We are running the risk of immobilizing a substantial portion of the world's wealth in someone's stamp collection."

(ii) Corporations and Institutions: As one moves from individual to group strategies in coping with inflation, the odds of optimality diminish. As economist Mancur Olson put it, "unless the number of individuals in a group is quite small, or unless there is coercion or some other special device to make individuals act in their common interest, rational, self-interested individuals will not act to achieve their common or group interests."

At the level of Corporations and Institutions, collective organizational survival in the 1970s usually depended upon transcending Defeatist and Free Rider strategies; inflation reinforced the normal conservative bias of organizations that favors the Maintenance Man and discourages the Entrepreneur in an environment calling for the opposite; corporate Maintenance strategies are short- to medium-term, aimed at quick profit turnover or to assure an increased market share for mature products; Maintenance strategies have a limited risk orientation focused on cost-benefit tradeoffs within the organization; Entrepreneurial corporate strategies stress long-term planning and investments in areas of greatest potential growth, focusing on maximizing the benefits or cutting costs through activities outside the organization. For example, Japanese manufacturers illustrate Entrepreneurial strategies compared to their "native" competition in the American and European markets.

The shift from more predictable, generally more stable growth rates of the 1950s and 1960s to the inflationary uncertainties and recessionary drops of the 1970s and 1980s called for a change in types of corporate strategy to meet the new environmental challenges. Many chief executives of corporations today were brought up in an era that emphasized caution over Entrepreneurship, that stressed the Maintenance caretaker objectives of short-term profit growth, good price-earning ratios and a stable return on investments or assets. The role of the chief executive as Entrepreneur is being replaced by his role as ring-master, while the line manager's traditional role of implementor and conservator is being reversed to that of Entrepreneur. Fred Gluck, chairman of McKinsey and Company's strategic management steering committee, maintains that the goal of planning in the present era is to shift thinking "away from methodology and toward clever, creative, insightful, and opportunistic decision-making to gain a competitive edge." The inflationary environment today, in short, calls for a redirection of corporate strategy from mere Maintenance thinking to Entrepreneurial thinking.

As William C. Norris, founder, chairman and chief executive officer of Control Data Corporation, noted: "Today's emphasis is on immediate payoffs from marginal improvement in existing offerings and from lower labor costs through mechanization and automation. In such an environment, it is no surprise that development of new products and services takes a back seat. But big business is not alone. It shares its apathetic, risk-avoiding, selfish, and reactionary profile with other sectors, including academia, organized labor, private foundations, the churches and government." The popularity of risk-avoidance in modern society recalls the prediction of Schumpeter that at advanced stages of development the capitalist economy undermines the vital entrepreneurial or innovative function as technological progress and the bureaucratic administration of large corporations transforms innovation itself into a routine matter and as committees and teams of experts are substituted for individual initiative.

The corporate strategies that do appear to cope with the conditions of stagflation most successfully are based on well-to-do and stable states, such as Japan and West Germany, where Maintenance functions in terms of restraining inflation can be taken for granted through a conservative political culture and effective state responsibility, freeing private (and "public") corporations from some of their own Maintenance costs so that they can focus more intensely upon Entrepreneurship and changing export markets. Thus, for example, five years ago Toyo Kogya, the Mazda automaking company based in Hiroshima, was faced with the threat of bankruptcy just as Chrysler and British Leyland are today: It was an overstaffed, mismanaged producer of gas-guzzling cars. The traditional loyalty of the Japanese local community, labor force and private creditors permitted the company to restructure and innovate so that by the 1980s the productivity rate was doubled, the debt cut in half and not a single worker was fired. Toyo Kogya successfully blended Maintenance and Entrepreneurial strategies, for example introducing robots while simultaneously guaranteeing that no one would lose a job, illustrating perhaps an optimum Western corporate policy in terms of inflation-fighting and technological advancement with minimum social cost.

(iii) The State: As one proceeds from individual portfolios to corporate strategies and from there to government policies, clear-cut private interests become increasingly obscure leaving an enigma behind called "the public good." Often Western state anti-inflation policies, which should be encouraging Entrepreneurship as a means of reversing declining productivity and economic growth rates, serve rather to add to the uncertainty, turning citizens into Defeatists and Free Riders and businesspeople into conservative Maintenance Men. Through Jacobinist promises to satisfy everyone's needs in the past, the Western democratic nation-state has increased the mystique of inflation and undermined its own legitimacy in the present. Indeed, some of the most successful strategies of individuals and private institutions have been based on the assumption that the government would never be able to keep its promises to control inflation and, therefore, one should either invest in inflation through hard assets or spread one's risks internationally in order to be able to play the effects of the few competent state anti-inflation policies against the many more numerous incompetent ones. One way many people did this in the 1970s was to buy German marks and Swiss francs, indirectly pushing the very reluctant Germans and Swiss in the direction of sponsoring international reserve currencies, partially displacing the discredited American dollar.

But the exceptional successes of West German and Swiss stabilization policies were anomalies, not models, depending upon extraordinary and (in part) extra-democratic prerequisites: great wealth, conservative Maintenance political cultures, social contracts capable of keeping polarization in check, a widespread anti-inflation consensus in the population, protective attitudes towards domestic markets threatened too closely, the ability to import and export foreign labor as needed, relative national homogeneity and limited geographical size.

(iv) <u>The International System</u>: In the era of flexible exchange rates, hard currency countries were able to pursue Entrepreneurial strategies within their Maintenance frameworks using the Euromarkets as "Free Riders" to reduce the costs of imported inflation. For example, West Germans won in the "floating game" by appreciating their currency to push down imported inflation, but not to the level of global inflation thus preserving their export markets. And the Austrians maintained a hard-currency policy and used foreign-exchange-rate-subsidized capital imports to finance domestic restructuring and development. The strategies of weak currency countries, on the other hand, aimed for mere Maintenance by using depreciation to improve their balance of current accounts and to substitute for imported depression or unemployment. But all these vicious-circle strategies are very expensive in terms of stimulating world inflation and the burdens for future domestic development when the foreign debt mortgages must be repaid. Hard currency countries support the so-called "workability" of a flexible system of exchange rates in which they are best able to improve their terms of trade through upward floating whereas a disproportionate share of the costs of the system via world inflation and deterioration of terms of trade seem to be borne domestically by the majority--the weak-currency states.

IV.

The ability of a nation to adapt effectively to the exogenous shocks of the 1970s depended upon patterns of both adapting and refusing to adapt to change as well as upon the state's bargaining power in the world economy. Except for oil producers, developing nations were forced into Defeatist and Free Rider strategies. Inflation preoccupied rich nations with something to lose and Western democracies became mired in Maintenance thinking which is ultimately self-defeating in an era requiring future-oriented, risk-taking Entrepreneurship. Fear of loss inspired a neo-conservative movement expressed in over-rationalistic, anti-inflation monetarist policies and in the priority of "order management" over "social justice," of reviving East-West conflicts instead of resolving North-South conflicts.

Nation-states may have their own life-cycles in terms of democratic attitudes towards socio-economic change which are reflected in shifts of private and public inflation strategies. In early industrialization, Entrepreneurial strategies displace Defeatist and Free-Rider patterns. In late industrialization, Maintenance-management strategies emerge. Public deficit financing then attempts to shift Entrepreneurial investment from the private to public sectors, associated with growing Maintenance bureaucracy; and Defeatist and Free-Rider strategies then become commonplace among displaced people in this recent "progressive phase" of welfare-state development.

Commentary*

I. Inflation, Hyper-Inflation and Security

Vera Zamagni: Do you think we need to distinguish between inflation and hyper-inflation and if so, where should we draw the line?

Hankel: Hyper-inflation occurs when private and public consumption (instead of investment) are financed through inflationary credits. Analytically, hyper-inflation is a consequence of non-investment financing. Examples can be found in the periods after the French Revolution, the First World War and the Second World War. Since hyper-inflation occurs principally as a result of wars and major crises, it cannot be found in "normal times" and does not apply to our current period.

Deutsch: In the economics sections of most of the world's major newspapers, armaments are generally treated as "confidence increasing." There are, however, a few economists like Kenneth Boulding who take a dim view of the stabilizing effects of armaments. Among political scientists there is a very widespread contention that arms races increase nothing so much as *in*security and that a country effectively loses power in the world when its share in the world population contributes to increased war efforts. An increased effort in armaments makes matters worse because it draws from the productive sector and adds to the unproductive sector as well as, in the long run, militarizing states. I notice here that economists and political scientists have less communication with each other than one might hope. Do economists generally feel that the increased military efforts do or do not increase security? How does an individual react to increasing military expenditures? Does he put his

---

*This represents a summary of the discussion at the April 30, 1981 Workshop, not direct quotation. The final editing of the Commentary to include the main points of the debate was completed with the able assistance of Ronald Bee, Janice Delbert and Wolfgang Schill. Space limitations have permitted only a sample of the taped discussion to be represented here in order to give a flavor of the dialogue.

savings into investments, a piggy bank, or a bank account?

Hager: Newspapers do not necessarily reflect the long-term reasoning of economists. It is, however, a fact that businessmen respond favorably to increased expenditures on arms, explainable by short-term demand effects. In addition where the market is sheltered, as it is with armaments, high profits can be made. For whatever reasons, there is a much more positive attitude towards increasing arms expenditures, as this will mean "good business."

Goldfield: It is fairly clear from both papers that there is an evident increase of uncertainty associated with a higher rate of inflation. Yet before the 1930s there was no economic policy at all; there was no unemployment insurance; there was no deposit insurance; there were no bailouts for large corporations. All these things have changed the nature of the world, created expectations and made it more difficult for governments to scare people to adjust their behavior. The question is how can you avoid going back to the 1930s and make progress towards controlling inflation while limiting social costs. Given the increased uncertainty caused by inflation and unemployment--plus the fact that you can't scare people like you could in the 1930s, more creative thought will be needed on reducing wages rather than solely relying on a framework of reduction of inflation by assertion.

Deutsch: You have touched upon a worrisome point which has concerned many political scientists. Namely, if one tries to go back to the economic policies of the 1930s--scaring people--one might get the political effects of the 1930s with the technology and weapons systems of the 1980s which seems to be an excellent recipe for global suicide.

II. Inflation as a Cause of Contradiction Between the Goals of Redistribution and Status-Quo Maintenance

Weisband: I believe there is a contradiction in Hankel's argument. On the one hand, there is the proposition that inflation is a useful tool of public policy and that governments do and should continue to use it in the future. But then in a different context I detect that Hankel is in fact accusing governments of acting fraudulently; that somehow this is not positive or at least is not what we ought to be experiencing under current economic and political circumstances. My question is simply, is there a contradiction, and if not, how not?

Hankel: There is a contradiction in the attitude of governments, but not in my paper. Governments, at least in democratic states, are looking to the majority vote. If the majority vote is against inflation because people fear losing value in their savings accounts or diminished purchasing power, then governments, to be elected, will always badmouth inflation. For the same society, however, inflation is clandestinely solving many distribution problems. Therefore, the contradiction lies not in my presentation, but rather in the actions of governments who criticize inflation while concurrently being happy with the results of inflation-generated redistribution.

III. Social Security, the Elderly and Influences on Risk-Taking

Goldfeld: In the United States, in spite of a 100% officially indexed social security system, inflation exacerbates the problems of the system rather than improving them. This occurs because, in times of declining real wages, the tax base which pays for the social security system rises essentially with nominal wages which in turn increase less rapidly than the social security benefits paid to citizens. The benefits expenditures increase in accordance with the price index and demographic problems can also worsen the tax revenue/benefit payments balance. As a result, the social security system in the U.S. has been a motivating force for trying to do something about inflation. It has not, however, solved the intergenerational problems that Hankel refers to.

Deutsch: In Hankel's paper it seems that instead of a demographic explosion of babies, we have a progressive explosion of oldsters. This would be a bit of a biological miracle. Those over 65 years old make up between 10 and 15% of the population. These "dangerous characters" used to have an average life expectancy of 68 years and now have one of somewhere between 73 and 74 years which means 6 more years of old people and a rough population increase of 7 to 8%. It is questionable whether this percentage can considerably alter the equilibrium of the overall economy. After all, one must also consider that between 10 and 25 years are needed to educate these people, to train them, or if they are untrained and unskilled, to keep them unemployed until they become so disillusioned that they are ready to work for little income. Nonetheless, the United States has done something simple to prevent bankruptcy of the social security system. A federal law has been passed which prohibits firing a worker for reasons of age before the age of 70. The elderly are on the average living five years longer (70-75), thereby taking more from social security funds while contributing to the fund for an additional five years (age 65-70). The law allows one to retire earlier but at a much lower benefit rate, proportional to when one retires. Generally, those with interesting and well paid jobs are delighted to work longer, while those with low-paying and uninteresting occupations retire earlier for less benefits.

Goldfeld: The United States currently has about three active workers per social security retiree, a reduction of the 5 to 1 ratio in 1960. Over the next 50 years this ratio will decline further to the point where there will be two active workers per retiree. Deutsch's 8% elderly growth rate figure is not accurate in terms of assessing the burden on existing workers to finance social security retirees.

Hankel: The American social security system does not accept age as a reason to fire people. This, however, is not the case in Germany. In the Federal Republic of Germany, older citizens can opt out of the labor market and receive 100% pension benefits if they retire before reaching the age of 62. What results is an increasing number of oldsters which burden the social security system with growing public budget deficits.

Hager: I must argue against Isaak's interpretation that a less insured society provides for more mobility and change. If true, then social insurance would negatively affect management's willingness to take risks and labor's willingness to tolerate change. In the 1960s, however, both Western Europe and Japan were highly insured, had a high rate of change and widespread risk-taking across the board. In fact, Japan had the most perfected insurance system in the business. The question of risk, adventure, and social security is therefore much more complex than has been indicated here.

Isaak: "Maintenance," as I have defined it, is a pattern of behavior which tends to keep up with the inflation rate while limiting risk-taking in order to do so. A fundamental psychological consideration in Western democracies is that inflation and growth also bring fears of losing value to large sectors of the population. The focus for these sectors shifts from entrepreneurial motivations to maintenance concerns because the cost of maintaining their present living standard has gone up. They have to work harder or get higher interest rates on their savings just to stay at the same standard of living. Through his article in International Organizations (Autumn 1980), Katzenstein illustrates how in Switzerland lower maintenance costs at home allow the Swiss to take higher entrepreneurial risks abroad. Such "aggressive adaptors" during the 1970s tended to have stable social systems with minimal political polarization. This description fit West Germany and Switzerland while hardly being applicable to Italy and France. Of course, political debate did take place in Germany and Switzerland, but it was not so polarized as to affect entrepreneurial risk-taking. It comes back to Deutsch's differing European North-South strategies and what we mean by capitalism in a particular context.

IV. The Meaning of Elite Change

Hankel: Schumpeter's analysis shows a connection between innovation, productivity and change in ruling classes. In Europe, and perhaps also in the U.S., innovations in products have been associated with the removal of elites. This, however, does not seem to be the case for Japan.

Deutsch: Do you think that the coming of the automobile age changed the ruling elite in the United States? Does it really matter to people when they choose presidents whether new products are on the market? Are there that many differences between the election of Howard Taft, Eisenhower, or Reagan that can be explained by the dynamics of innovation and productivity? Has the elite changed that much?

Isaak: Perhaps due to the lack of feudal tradition in the United States, one could argue that no one, including Henry Kissinger, really has the feeling of ever having "made it." In America, upward mobility is insatiable, tending to boost innovation because whenever people reach the top of the mountain, it's still not high enough. This results in relatively wealthy people leading productive lives and not resting on the laurels of status. During the 1970s, however, the situation in the U.S. developed in the direction of a more class-based, class-consolidated society in which mobility was limited. Deutsch wrote an interesting article in 1975 (in International Studies Quarterly) on the images of scarcity and the difficulties which can occur when one believes too much in the inevitability of scarcity and the limits of growth as a negative self-fulfilling prophecy. In fact, the 1970s witnessed growing insecurity about inflation, prices, wages, and employment which resulted in a certain neoconservatism, focusing more on the concrete. People concentrated more on their own wage and its devaluation, their own bargaining power, their own purchasing power, and their own job security. This naturally leads to a conservative consolidation of the existing class structure. It also leads to more interest in maintenance strategies and less interest in entrepreneurial strategies.

V. Price Levels, Price Structure and Redistribution

Stefano Zamagni: It has hitherto been forgotten that inflation, and thus the change in price levels, is not a situation with a constant rise of all prices, but rather a distortion, over time, of the relative price structure. The fact that some prices climb quicker than others implies redistribution effects and changes in the structure of capital. It is not at all clear whether the redistribution effects or the new capital structure would be preferred. The idea that inflation is not dangerous--the main thesis of today's discussion--assumes that if future prices are correctly anticipated, then any set of future prices will be equitable since present prices will adapt to expected future prices. For this to be true, it is not enough to correct the anticipated general price level at the old rate. It is also necessary to correctly anticipate the whole structure of relative prices, something which is impossible to accept unless we introduce the assumption of perfect foresight. Thus, the effect of inflation depends on the capability on the part of economic agents to be able to anticipate correctly the whole structure of relative prices. Even if one wants to have the beneficial effects of inflation, it is not enough to anticipate a continuous rate of inflation. One would have to anticipate a continuous increase in the rate of inflation. At this point, distinction between expectation and anticipation is necessary. Expectation is a state of mind whereas anticipation refers to actual behavior. Redistributive effects in terms of productive resources cannot be anticipated because if they are fully and completely anticipated, then we don't effectively have a redistribution effect. It is thus most improbable that all the effects of inflation can be fully anticipated.

Hankel: There are psychologically dangerous aspects of the politics of stabilization with or without an official index of the demand for money. People misinterpret stability as an abstraction of the general price level, that the real purchasing power of their demand for money should act as solid insurance against changes in their share of real income and wealth. They confuse the stability of price levels with the stability of relative prices and income, which no one can guarantee. This, as Schumpeter points out, essentially depends on who is in power and on monopolists. A price-setter changes, with his price, the price-structure, namely his price in relation to other prices. The fight against inflation does not switch off the power struggle over relative prices; it intensifies it.

VI. Costs of Inflation, Costs of Inflation-Fighting and Oligopolies

Goldfeld: Hankel's paper contains two main points: one is a rather gloomy notion that there are no reliable methods to fight inflation--that is the bad news; and then the good news is that it doesn't matter much, because the damages of inflation are overrated and in fact there are some positive things about inflation. This latter view is, to some extent, contradicted by Isaak's paper which documents some of the costs of inflation as evidenced by degrees of social uncertainty and confusion. This uncertainty, in turn, affects investments, savings, and the efficiency of the price mechanism. There are other problems as well. In the U.S. the tax system is decidedly non-neutral in terms of its impact on inflation. Given the way the tax system works, some of the reactions to inflation in the U.S. are real reactions to the indirect effect of taxation that inflation induces. There are other costs associated with inflation: capricious income redistribution, institutions whose existence depend on a non-inflationary environment are threatened, and financial systems which have interest rates ceilings are obviously affected. There is a whole contracting process between labor and management whose viability is endangered by inflationary pressures. Inflation also calls into question all kinds of accounting practices. Normal measures of the public sector deficit are distorted rather badly by inflation. Firms which have outstanding debts valued in nominal terms suddenly reap large capital gains whenever there is substantial inflation, but repay in deflated dollars. We don't measure inflation very well which also adds complications. What this all means is that perhaps inflation does have more serious costs than Hankel has alluded to. In addition, to adopt a laissez-faire attitude towards inflation does not guarantee good economic performance. If we ignore the costs of inflation, how do we sensibly go about looking for a public policy strategy that balances those costs in a realistic way?

Deutsch: What might happen if people were no longer frightened by unemployment and were no longer willing to accept lower wages? This would, of course, depend on the degree of a society's organization. By 1981, the better part of European and overseas labor has been organized. Bureaucratic military state machineries are in place, tending to increase the cost of producing goods. By the year 2000 it is feasible that everyone's output in the world market will be of a monopolistic or oligopolistic nature. The oligopoly of labor can more readily be broken at the national level since on the international level oligopolistic pressures are not as detectable and cannot be forcibly resolved at anybody's expense. Does this mean we are moving toward a cost-push inflation or, through the spread of organizational capabilities and the growing bureaucratization of states, toward the multilateral oligopolization of export prices in the world?

Goldfeld: Oligopolistic influences on inflation rates are far from clear-cut. The only clear message from economic theory is that oligopolies lead to higher prices and less competition. There is little evidence which supports the idea that oligopolies are capable of generating inflation indefinitely. One cannot, of course, distinguish higher prices from inflation. If the world is totally oligopolized, then the process stops and one has to ask what else causes inflation. It's not just going to be oligopolies.

*Coe: It is not clear that an increase in the degree of oligopoly has only unfavorable implications for inflation performance. Indeed large centralized labor and employer organizations may facilitate the successful implementation of incomes policies. Germany and Austria are examples where agreements between labor, employers, and the government have played an important role in maintaining inflation at a low level. By contrast, the United States may lack the necessary institutions to implement such incomes policies.

Hager: If it were true the world would become a great oligopoly in the year 2000, it would be the best thing that could happen to us, for two historical reasons: first, the experience of the European economy in the 1960s which was oligopolistically oriented--little foreign competition, cooperation of labor, firms competing according to oligopolistic rules--which was initially associated with high growth and low inflation; and second, the pattern of mutual contractual payments among different social groups established during this same period which was compatible with full employment. The European experience in the 1960s was unique; it has never been achieved before or since.

Hankel: Inflation, oligopoly and changes in relative prices have brought about changes in both cost and output structures which encourage innovation and substitution. OPEC's monopolistic escalation of oil prices was only one example. Without the oil price hikes we would neither have the oil substitute from the North Sea nor the current lucrative forms of alternative energy sources. Xeno-credit markets make for another impressive example. Their recycling effect not only made the carrying out and financing of the high OPEC oil prices possible, but also was responsible--to OPEC's displeasure--for the generation of alternative energy forms. Given this example, Deutsch's vision of the oligopolization of world business becomes less frightening. This confirms Schumpeter's thesis of automatic, self-correcting forces of "productive" inflation financing, also demonstrating the financing of technical innovation. The only frightening thing one observes is the "dual inflation morality" of government officials. For example, the

*These comments and those following are the personal observations of David Coe and do not represent the official position of the OECD.

West German finance minister, who at home is anti-inflation, nonetheless takes giant credits from the Saudis in order to plug a hole in his budget. There is nothing wrong with that per se but he, instead of publicly bombasting inflation, should be advocating the need of foreign capital to finance the domestic goal of full employment.

Coe: Professor Hankel is concerned that the attempt to reduce inflation is worse than the disease; that is, the cure risks killing the patient, not the germ. But it is not clear whether a laissez-faire policy towards inflation will lead to stabilization and not hypertrophy. The real danger of inflation is the possibility of it accelerating: you feel you can live with inflation if it just doesn't get worse. The public is right to question whether a government which cannot stabilize prices can stabilize inflation. But if we are not going to fight inflation to its death, do we not at least have to do something? Certain simple monetarist solutions appear to be very expensive both in terms of social and economic costs. We should not ignore that there have been national policies for controlling inflation that have been quite successful, even in the United States.

Weisband: The following three points are central to the problem of inflation and constitute the core of Hankel's argument: First, the point that oligopolies compete for innovation. I would here introduce the name of Kondratieff to complement Schumpeter's analysis. The entire Hankel argument revolves around presumptions of scarcity, as evidenced by a series of cycles. The first question is thus, what is the role of the public sector in encouraging innovation? In particular, what is the relationship between government (or public bureaucracy) and large corporations (or private bureaucracy)? Each nation has its own relationship--Japan's is different from England's, and so on--but each still must determine its relationship in terms of expenditures and innovation. Second, an innovation that must occur is innovation in the energy sector. To what degree will the public sector support innovation in energy substitution and how fast will that competition occur in terms of increasing productivity to deal with both scarcity and the consequential inflationary impact? In fact, the promotion of modern innovations is a strategy consisting of a mixture of risks and costs. So as the welfare state insures a part of private life-risks, we require a new fulcrum of risk-understanding between the state and the market. Third, what is the role of the state in terms of the internationalization of capital? Hankel is perhaps making too much of the consequences of the Euromarket, of Eurocurrency, and of the xeno-market in terms of undermining the traditional role of the state as authority. There is a suggestion that the Eurocurrency market was a sinister, inflationary force which made national income policies virtually superfluous.

Hankel: Did I say sinister?

Weisband: In other words, we may well be dealing with an international process in which there is a rising division of labor that increasingly will create domestic problems for individual states. The state, to the contrary, will increasingly become more important for solving future conflicts.

VII. Inflation and the North/South Discussion

Aker: There has been one element that has been conspicuously absent in this discussion of inflation, namely the distribution of goods and income between the North and the South. Inflation has been an institutional response, combined with an appreciation of currencies in the North, to resist the redistribution of income in favor of the South. In the final analysis, inflation is a monetary question and sooner or later the increases in prices are connected to an increase in the money supply. It is clear that by holding the money supply at an appropriate level or within an appropriate increment, you can manage the price level and reduce prices. It is a fact that the North does not want to reduce prices. Additionally, the fact that prices are increasing at a less rapid rate in the parts of the North where we have appreciation of currencies is indication of a willingness to withhold the delivery of goods to the oil producers or to other countries whose terms of trade are improving.

Hankel: Since there is a flexible exchange rate, we have a different situation concerning the relations between North and South. Different rates of inflation, through exchange adjustments, can be balanced.

Weisband: Is it true that Third World countries with the highest inflation rates are further advanced in their domestic development than others?

Aker: This seems very doubtful. The grounds for inflation in developing countries usually lie in high state deficits and subsidies in the private sector. Therefore, this would not be good development policy.

Hankel: Nevertheless, inflation in developing countries has not been altogether harmful in building a more efficient domestic structure.

Aker: I beg to differ......

Hankel: Today's newly industrializing countries (NICs) have had high inflation rates for over ten years: Mexico, Brazil, Taiwan, Korea, etc.

VIII. Taxation as a Means of Promoting Innovation

Isaak: Goldfeld has advocated a tax-based income policy. This is based on the feasibility that the U.S. Congress would accept and not oppose a legislative attempt to use the tax system to hold pay increases to 5% per annum when the rate of inflation is twice that rate.

Deutsch: In other words, the unions would agree to a 5% reduction?

Goldfeld: No, no. First, the target wage rate need not be chosen to be absurdly low. Second, the policy would be voluntary but provide incentives for good wage behavior. For example, it could work by increasing the corporate tax rate on businesses which actually offer large wage increases. This is called the backbone approach. You give corporations backbone to resist wage increases. This is probably politically unacceptable. The only politically acceptable approach would be the positive one, not a penalty but a reward approach, which would give tax credits for good wage performance.

Aker: What would you do with the money supply in the meantime?

Goldfeld: You would do the same thing that you would be doing otherwise. You would not change one bit the control of aggregate demand. Such an income policy serves to make the short-term effects of the respective monetary and fiscal policies more agreeable, i.e. to have less of a depressing effect on real income and employment.

Aker: Have we not seen some evidence which suggests that the distribution of income within a country is almost structural? So that if through one trick or another you can convince the workers to take a lower wage this year than the next year, chances are that once you exhaust your tricks they'll come back with demands of a nature which will try to restore the original structural distribution.

Coe: But one now has quite a restrictive monetary policy in the U.S. and this is what Goldfeld advocates continuing in conjunction with the tax-based incomes policy. Since the Nixon era we know that we can't crank up the economy while concurrently trying to hold down prices and wages with controls. There's got to be consistency between the two.

IX. Contradictions Between the Two Papers

Deutsch: We were told by Hankel that, according to Schumpeter and Wicksell, inflation tends to promote innovation by making credit available. Isaak has told us that inflationary periods seem to stimulate conservative mentalities. Apparently, either a distinction needs to be made or there is a contradiction.

Isaak: The difficulty is in the historical context. To look at inflation in the 1970s, one finds that advanced Western societies are in a post-industrial phase with high inflation rates, falling productivity growth rates, falling innovation, falling investment in technology--except for a handful of countries like Japan, France and Germany. There's not necessarily a contradiction--it just happens to be that at this particular historical moment there is high inflation at the same time as a conservative reaction caused by the general uncertainty stemming from a sense of decline of the West, the break-up of the monetary system, and a general sense of insecurity that happens to be perhaps military and strategic as much as it is economic.

Hankel: Our society is switching from an investor's mentality to a saver's mentality. The contradictions lie less in our papers and more in daily economic realities. An economy with exclusively a saver's mentality simply cannot survive. This is where Isaak's typification of behavior patterns can be very helpful.

Aker: Are there more than four categories of behavior patterns?

Isaak: These categories are certainly not exhaustive; they do fall into the mode of Weberian ideal types which seem clearest on the individual strategic level. At the corporate strategy level, however, a certain Olsonian paradox makes for more complications. When the collective state level of decision-making is reached, it often becomes difficult to distinguish between the private and public interest. Problems arise with the unanticipated consequences of using these categories--which does not mean that people will not use such categories or that they are not useful.

Goldfeld: There is a methodological problem which is to relate the ideal types on the individual behavioral level to corporate and state behaviors. A logical step should be from some sort of basis of psychological literature why these are the sort of universal human reactions to uncertainty. There is an analogy in economic literature which is Professor Tobin's original discussion of portfolio theory which distinguished between a variety of attitudes toward risk. He called them risk-lovers, risk-averters, plungers, etc.

Deutsch: Tobin is a highly respected economist. And I am pleased to notice here a paper matching this legitimate methodological approach. What Isaak has attempted to do is the following. He observed what certain individuals did to try to cope with the inflation of the 1970s and organized the results in four categories. Then he examined the behavior of corporations and states during the same period in black-box fashion, without concerning himself with their inner structures,to determine what kinds of similarities the input-output behavior of these units had with the four categories of individual behavior. That is a very interesting thing to do! Larger systems can behave like smaller ones just as states can be exactly as aggressive in their behavior as the individuals are who lead them. Hitler's Germany is a perfect example. Both the behavior of the individual and of the state he governed were nasty and aggressive. Such a distribution of psychological types that can be applied at different levels may take us methodologically beyond the complicated theories of Erik Erickson, enabling social scientists to do a kind of market research analysis: for example, a state or corporation might be in the market for a maintenance man in a certain historical phase--supported by people who, themselves, may not be conservative. In the future Isaak could establish the information and resource prerequisites for the different types he has uncovered. What he is doing is quite consistent with a good deal of social science.

X. Closing Remarks

Hankel: We all agree that there is inflation, but where does it come from and where does it lead? I realized today that the nature of inflation is complicated, yet the problems of inflation and its dangers, in my opinion, are overrated. Fighting against inflation can cause as many forms of damage as inflation itself. Schumpeter's analysis of the financing of innovation through inflationary credit mechanisms reinforces my point. As does the element of self-correcting forces in inflation. I also learned that there is a new sensitivity in our rich, egalitarian welfare society because when people are wealthier they are more afraid of losing something......

Deutsch: There seems to be a contradiction......

Hankel: Agreed. Because interest groups are against the collective interest. Because savers' interests increase over investors' interests, because no one wants to lose anything--no adjustments are being made. The only paradox is that inflation continues and will strengthen. Investors must outwit savers. Unions, the defenders of real wages, will have to confront either higher inflation or higher unemployment rates (or both). If we can't fight inflation effectively, then it would be better to accept inflation or have a better stabilization of prices as a goal of political economy. Yes, we can accept the terms of inflation.

Isaak: My comments are in the same direction. I would first agree with Goldfeld that what I have offered are four descriptive categories after the fact. The real question is whether certain combinations of these descriptive categories do have explanatory capacities for behavior patterns in terms of the reaction to economic uncertainty. The question is not whether these particular categories are useful, but rather if these are not used, then which alternative concepts are more accurate in describing modern reactions to inflation. The question is more fundamental than Hager's methodological hesitations about the links between inflation and uncertainty. At a certain point, the individual or the social scientist is in the dilemma of Buridan's donkey starving between two bales of hay. He can deliberately choose one bail or another to try and solve his dilemma. You have to start somewhere. Each political scientist, economist, or political economist must choose his own concept and test it. Inflation is a complex problem. Much too complex to leave to either political scientists, or economists, or politicians alone. It concerns all individuals in everyday life who walk around with a wallet full of paper money.

Deutsch: Thank you very much. I have learned from our discussion today and thank the participants for their conscientious participation.

BIBLIOGRAPHY

Aliber, R.Z. (ed.). National Monetary Policies and the International Financial System. Chicago and London: University of Chicago Press, 1974.

American Economic Review, articles on the interest rate/anticipated inflation debate, June and September issues of 1982.

Bach, George. The New Inflation: Causes, Effects, Cures. Providence, R.I.: Brown University Press, 1972.

Bach, G.L. and Stephenson, James B. "Inflation and the Redistribution of Wealth," in Review of Economics and Statistics, Vol. 56, February 1974, pp. 1-13.

Becker, Gary. "A Theory of the Allocation of Time," Economic Journal, September 1965.

Block, Fred L. The Origins of International Economic Disorder. Berkeley, Ca.: University of California Press, 1977.

Brandt, Willy et al. North-South: A Programme for Survival. Cambridge, Ma.: MIT Press, 1980.

Branson, W.H. Macroeconomic Theory. N.Y.: Macmillan, 1972.

Brems, Hans. Inflation, Interest and Growth. Lexington, Ma.: Lexington, 1980.

Brillembourg, Arturo. "The Dynamics of Inflation: Forward Contracts and Money," IMF Staff Papers, Vol. 26, Nr. 24, Dec. 1979.

Bronfenbrenner, M. and Holzman, F.D. "A Survey of Inflation," in American Economic Review, Vol. 53 (4), pp. 593-661.

Cairncross, Alec. Inflation, Growth and International Finance. London: George Allen and Unwin, 1975.

Claassen, E.M. Weltinflation. Münich, 1978.

Claassen, E.M. (ed.). Kompendium der Währungstheorie. Münich: 1977.

Claassen, E.M. "Zins und Inflation: Bemerkungen zu einer Synthese der Wicksellschen und Fisherschen Inflationstheorie," Zeitschrift für Nationalökonomie, 34 (1974).

Celio, N. (ed.) Inflationsbekämpfung unter veränderten wirtschaftlichen und sozialen Bedingungen. Bern-Stuttgart, 1976.

Cohen, Benjamin. Organizing the World's Money. N.Y.: Basic Books, 1977.

Dahrendorf, Ralf. Lebenschancen. Frankfurt: Suhrkamp Verlag, 1979.

Davenport, John A. "A Testing Time for Monetarism," Fortune, October 6, 1980.

Deutsch, Karl. "Limited Growth and Continuing Inequality," Chapter 17 in Tides Among Nations. New York: The Free Press, 1979.

Dougherty, Thomas. Controlling the New Inflation. Lexington, Ma.: Lexington, 1981.

Ehrlicher, W. and Becker, W.D. (ed.) Die Monetarismus-Kontroverse, Beihefte zu Kredit und Kapital, Heft 4, Berlin, 1978.

Fautz, W. "Verteilungskampfhypothesen der Inflation. Eine kritische Übersicht," Schweizerische Zeitschrift für Volkswirtschaft und Statistik, 114 (1978).

Flanders, M. Development in an Inflationary World. N.Y.: Academic Press, 1981.

Friedman, Milton (ed.) Studies in the Quantity Theory of Money. Chicago: University of Chicago Press, 1956.

Friedman, Milton. Unemployment versus Inflation?: An Evaluation of the Phillips Curve, in Occasional Paper 44 of the Institute of Economic Affairs. London: 1975.

Friedman, Milton. Tax Limitation, Inflation and the Role of Government. Dallas: Fisher Institute, 1978.

Frisch, H. Neue Inflationstheorie. Goettingen: Vandenhoeck and Ruprecht, 1980.

Frisch, H. "Inflation Theory 1963-1975: A "Second Generation" Survey," Journal of Economic Literature XV 4, December 1977.

Gordon, W.M. Inflation, Exchange Rates and the World Economy. Chicago: University of Chicago Press, 1977.

Haberler, Gottfried. "Two Essays on the Future of the International Monetary Order," Economic Quarterly Review, Number 7, June 1974.

Hall, Robert. Inflation: Causes & Effects. Chicago: University of Chicago Press, 1983.

Hicks, J.R. The Crisis in Keynesian Economics. Oxford: Blackwell, 1974.

Hirsch, Fred and Goldthorpe, John. The Political Economy of Inflation. Cambridge, Mass., 1978.

Hirsch, Fred. The Social Limits to Growth. London: Routledge Kegan Paul, 1978.

Hudson, John. Inflation: A Theoretical Synthesis. Winchester, Mass.: Allen & Unwin, 1982.

Johnson, H.G. Inflation and the Monetary Controversy. Amsterdam, 1972.

Johnson, H.G. "Secular Inflation and the International Monetary System" in JMCB, Vol. 5 (I), pp. 509-520.

Jones, Aubrey. The New Inflation: The Politics of Prices and Incomes. London: André Deutsch, 1973.

Katsushito, Iwai. Disequilibrium Dynamics: A Theoretical Analysis of Inflation and Unemployment. New Haven, Connecticut: Yale University Press, 1981.

Katzenstein, Peter J. "Capitalism in One Country?: Switzerland in the International Economy," International Organization, Vol. 34, Nr. 4, Fall 1980, pp. 507-540.

Keohane, Robert O. "The International Politics of Inflation," paper prepared for the Brookings Project on the Politics and Sociology of Global Inflation (mimeographed), September 1978.

Keynes, J.M. _A Treatise on Money_, Vol. II: _The Applied Theory of Money_. London: Macmillan, 1930.

Keynes, J.M. _The General Theory of Employment, Interest and Money_. London: Macmillan, 1936.

Keynes, J.M. "How to Pay for the War," in _The Collected Writings of John Maynard Keynes_, Vol. IX, _Essays in Persuasion_. London: Macmillan, 1972.

Khan, Mohsin. "Inflation and International Reserves: A Time-Series Analysis," _IMF Staff Papers_, Vol. 26, No. 4, December 1979.

Klaus, J. (with N. Müller). _Inflationstheorie_. Darmstadt, 1974.

Kleinewefers, H. _Inflation und Inflationsbekämpfung in der Schweiz_. Frauenfeld, 1976.

Krause, Lawrence and Salant, Walter S. (ed.) _Worldwide Inflation: Theory and Recent Experience_. Washington, D.C.: Brookings Institute, 1977.

Laidler, D.W. _Essays on Money and Inflation_. Manchester and Chicago: Manchester University Press and Chicago University Press, 1975.

Laidler, D. and Parkin, M. "Inflation: A Survey," _The Economic Journal_, 85, December 1975, pp. 709-809.

Lal, Depak. _Unemployment and Wage Inflation in Industrial Economies_, Paris: OECD, 1977.

Lekachman, Robert. _Inflation: The Permanent Problem of Boom and Bust_. N.Y.: Random House, 1973.

Levinson, Charles. _Capital, Inflation and the Multinationals_. London: Allen and Unwin, 1971.

Linder, Staffan Burenstam. _The Harried Leisure Class_. New York: Columbia University Press, 1970.

Lindberg, Leon. Inflation and Political Change. New York: Pergamon, 1980.

Lohr, Steve. "Making It in 1980: Inflation Rewrites Rules," The New York Times National Recruitment Survey, October 12, 1980.

Lovett, William. Inflation and Politics. Lexington, Ma.: Lexington, 1982.

Lundberg, E. (ed.) Inflation Theory and Anti-Inflation Policy. London: Macmillan, 1977.

Maital, S. "Inflation, Taxation and Equity," Economic Journal, 82 (325), March 1972, pp. 159-167.

Maneval, H. Die Phillips-Kurve: Empirische, theoretische und wirtschaftspolitische Aspekte, Tübingen: 1973.

Medley, Richard (ed.) The Politics of Inflation. New York: Pergamon Press, 1982.

Müller, N. Anspruchsverhalten sozialer Gruppen und Inflation. Köln: 1976.

Mundell, R.A. Monetary Theory: Inflation, Interest and Growth in the World Economy. Pacific Palisades, Calif.: 1971.

Newlyn, W.T. and Bootle, R.P. Theory of Money. Oxford: Clarendon Press, 1978.

O'Brien, D.P. The Classical Economists. Oxford; Clarendon Press, 1975.

OECD. Economic Outlook 26, December 1979. Paris: OECD, 1979.

OECD. United States: OECD Economic Survey. Paris: August 1980.

Okun, Arthur, Fowler, Henry and Gilber, Milton. Inflation: The Problems it Creates and the Policies it Requires. New York: New York University Press, 1970.

Okun, Arthur and Perry, George (eds.) Curing Chronic Inflation. Washington, D.C.: The Brookings Institute, 1978.

Perkins, J.O. Unemployment, Inflation and New Macroeconomic Policy. New York: St. Martin's Press, 1982.

Phillips, A.W. "The Relationship between Unemployment and the Rate of Change on Money Wage Rates in the U.K. 1861-1957," in Economics (NS), Vol. 25 (100), pp. 283-299.

Pütz, T. (ed.) Studien zum Inflationsproblem. Berlin: 1975.

Rahmann, B. "Inflation, Arbeitslosigkeit und Einkommensverteilung in der Bundesrepublik Deutschland 1960-1976," Kredit und Kapital 10 (1977).

Rocard, Michel and Gallus, Jacques. L'Inflation au Coeur. Paris: Gallienard, 1975.

Schumpeter, Joseph A. Kapitalismus, Sozialismus und Demokratie. München: Leo Lehnen Verlag GmbH, 1950.

Schumpeter, J.A. The Theory of Economic Development. Cambridge, Ma.: 1955.

Siebke, J. and Willms, M. "Zinsniveau, Geldpolitik und Inflation," Kredit und Kapital, 5 (1972).

Steinmann, Gunter. Inflationstheorie. Paderborn: 1979.

Streissler, E., Beinsen, L., Schleicher, St., Suppanz, H. Zur Relativierung des Zieles der Geldwertstabilität. Göttingen: 1976.

Streissler, E. Die schleichende Inflation als Phänomen der Pölitischen Ökonomie. Zürich: Basler Wirtschaftswissenschaftliche Vorträge, 1973.

Trevithick, J.A. "Keynes, Inflation and Money Illusion," Economic Journal, 85 (337), 1975, pp. 101-113.

Trevithick, J.A. Inflation. Middlesex: Penguin, 1977.

Weber, Max. The Methodology of the Social Sciences, edited by E. Shils and H.A. Finch. New York: The Free Press, 1949.

Weber, Max. Economy and Society. New York: Bedminster Press, 1968.

Weintraub, Sidney. Capitalism's Inflation and Unemployment Crisis. Reading, Ma.: Addison-Wesley, 1978.

Whitney, Simon. Inflation Since 1945. New York: Praeger, 1982.

Wicksell, Knut. Geldzins und Güterpreise (berichtigter Nachdruck der Ausgabe Jena 1898). Aalen: 1968.

Williams, Charles. Runaway Inflation: The Onset. New York: Theodor Gaus' Sons, 1972.

Willms, M. "Monetäre Zwischenziele europäischer Zentralbanken," Wirtschaftsdienst 58 (1978).

Willms, M. "Der Inflationsprozess in der Bundesrepublik und die Geldpolitik der Bundesbank," in Cassel, D., Gutmann, G., Thieme, H.J. (eds.) 25 Jahre Marktwirtschaft in der Bundesrepublik Deutschland. Stuttgart, 1972.

Wolfgang, Marvin (ed.) Social Effects of Inflation. Philadelphia: American Academy of Political and Social Science, 1981.

Woll, A. (ed.) Inflation: Definitionen, Ursachen, Wirkungen und Bekämpfungsmöglichkeiten. München: 1979.

Woll, A., Faulwasser, B., Ramb, B. Th. Beschäftigung, Geld und Preisniveaustabilität. Opladen: 1977.

Versluysen, Eugène L. The Political Economy of International Finance. New York: St. Martin's Press, 1981.

Ziercke, M. Die redistributiven Wirkungen von Inflationen. Göttingen, 1970.

ABOUT THE AUTHORS

Wilhelm Hankel was Director of the Department of Money and Credit in the Bonn Economic and Finance Ministry under Economics Minister Karl Schiller as of 1968. He was President of the Hessischen Landesbank in Frankfurt from 1972 through 1974. He has since served as Consultant to the European Commission in Brussels, to the Austrian, Saudi Arabian and South Korean governments, and has taught at Harvard, Georgetown and Johns Hopkins. Presently he is a Senior Economist at the International Institute for Management at the Science Center in Berlin. His most important books include *Wahrungspolitik* (1972), *Weltwirtschaft* (1977) and *Prosperity Amidst Crisis: Austria's Economic Policy and the Energy Crunch* (1980).

Robert Isaak has taught at the Johns Hopkins School of Advanced International Studies, New York University, SUNY at Purchase, and Pace University, where he presently teaches international organization and international management as Associate Professor of Management. His books include: *Politics for Human Beings* (with Ralph Hummel) (1975 and 1980), *Individuals and World Politics* (1975 and 1981), *American Democracy and World Power* (1977), and *European Politics: Political Economy and Policy Making in Western Democracies* (1980). He was a Senior Research Associate and Fellow at the West European Institute and Research Institute on International Change at Columbia University (1975-78), and completed this work with Hankel when on a three-year leave from Pace at the Johns Hopkins SAIS Bologna Center (1978-1981).

UNIVERSITY OF BRISTOL
28 AUG 2025
WITHDRAWN

UNIVERSITY OF BRISTOL

30110K
1003257999
84 18352